A MODEST SUMMATION OF THINGS

by
Robert Rahula

ALSO BY ROBERT RAHULA

NOVELS:
Messieurs
Panamaniac
Island of Misfits
Day Another Paradise In
One Last Fling
Bathhouse Stories
Conversation in a Belgian Bar
All the Yage in Reno
Exigent Circumstances
Uninvited Guest

POETRY:
Trigger Points
Dentro Del Corazón Bloqueada
Camino
Migration
I Sing the Body Politic
Wonderland
From Whose Bourn
Poemas Españoles
Expat Poems

ANTHOLOGIES:
Half Life
The Essential Dan Landes
Horror Stories for Children

A MODEST SUMMATION OF THINGS

© 2019 by Robert Rahula

All rights reserved. This book or any portion thereof may not be reproduced or used in any manner whatsoever without the express written permission of the author except for the use of brief quotations in a book review.

www.robertrahula.com

This is a work of fiction. Characters, organizations, businesses, products, locales, and events portrayed in this book either are products of the author's imagination or are used fictitiously.

ISBN 978-1-7329708-3-0

Alma-gator Press
Barcelona • Madrid • La Chorrera

dedicated to Carolina

... Y yo me iré.
Y se quedarán los pájaros cantando.

—Juan Ramon Jimenez
El Viaje Definitivo

CHAPTER ONE: VILLA ROSARIO

There is a certain smell to urine—have you noticed?—that tells you whether you are sick or well. As humans, our senses are particularly keen on smells.

Lately, my senses are telling me that death is coming.

Intuition is not a mysterious thing. It's comprised of hundreds of nano-details, like a whiff of urine, which the brain combines with hundreds of other details occurring in the same timeframe, and compares them to its entire lifelong catalog of memories, like the smell of dead people; the smell of dead animals; the smell of hospitals; the smell of morgues; the smell of peat; the smell of vomit; the smell of dog shit from sick dogs; the smell of rotting garbage. The brain then contrasts them with a million other opposite smells, like the smell of flowers; the smell of fresh water; the smell of healthy babies; the smell of air after a rain, the smell of happy people... and as the evidence mounts somewhere deep in the subconscious, the brain releases a few "floater" thoughts that rise up to the surface of awareness, like one or two tiny bubbles on an otherwise smooth pond, and then—if you're paying attention, or rather, if you are not distracted—you suddenly form the thought, as I did this morning while peeing into the toilet... that death is coming... not immediately, but soon... like the journey of a thousand miles, when you realize that you are further down the road that you thought, and there in the attainable future, visible in the mist, are the iron gates that will open and swallow you, and then shut tight.

It's easy to dismiss intuition. It takes so little, just the tiniest bit of derision, just a smidgeon of so-called common sense and the intuitive thought will evaporate as quickly "as a dream dies on the opening day" as the old hymn goes. And millions of people dismiss their intuition every day, as they climb into the car that will be crushed by a semi-truck as they drive to work that morning; as they take that early morning jog along the path that leads to their rape and murder; as they finish eating those oysters they ordered at the restaurant that will propel them to the hospital in six hours; because, after all, they had ordered them and they were expensive; and, after all, they had to get to work somehow; and, after all, they had jogged that same path for months without any problems....

I am not a superstitious man... well, no, that's not true... but let's just say I'm not an overly-superstitious man. In fact, those who claim to know me would say I am excessively rational, almost to a fault. Of course, they do not really know me. But what I am, statistically speaking, is an *old* man. And so, statistically speaking, I am on solid ground to say that sooner rather than later I shall be under that same solid ground... or burnt to ash and scattered to the wind.

And so... after peeing this morning, I decided to go to Europe. Why not? If I am going to die soon, I'd like to see Europe one more time. It seemed like a logical thought progression to me, completely rational. If A, then B. If you are going to die, why not take some money and go see Europe again, one last time? You can't spend that money when you're dead. I enjoy Europe—as a tourist, that is. I enjoy visiting new places. When you are a visitor, your senses are alive. Any location becomes mundane if you live there. But as a tourist, every place is exciting. That's how one should enjoy any place—as a tourist. And maybe that's how one should enjoy people as well—as a tourist. Maybe that's all I've been my whole life—just a tourist.

Thoreau recommended that a person live free and uncommitted as long as possible. But I don't know. I have done that. I have done exactly that... and I am free of wives or children or dependents or constraints or relationships or lifelong friends. I have been a tourist to my own life.

But Thoreau also said that every writer should be called upon to give a reckoning of his or her own life. And I do think that's true. And you can't do that after you die, either. You have to do that while you're still alive.

And so, I suppose that if I am to be called upon to give a reckoning before I go to Europe, that I should provide a little background. After all, you can't describe where you are going if you don't first know where you've been. Or maybe it's the other way around—that you can't understand where you come from until you know where you're going... At any rate, my name is Ricardo Mendes. I live alone, in a small studio apartment in Villa Rosario in Panama. When I first moved here, more than fifteen years ago, Villa Rosario was a quiet village, with dirt roads, spotty electricity, and certainly no WiFi. It has grown to almost six thousand people now, unfortunately, because so many gringos have moved here. They have come here to hide out, to recuperate from the trauma of the US culture, to disappear, or to reinvent themselves, or simply to have a quiet place to wait for death. But there are too many gringos here now. And gringos ruin everything. I try and avoid most of them down here, but that is becoming more difficult to do. I may have to move soon.

But for the moment, I still live in the same

apartment I rented when I first moved here. It's tiny, but I like the view. In fact, I love the view. It's why I stay, even though the apartment is only one room with a bed, a bathroom, and a kitchenette with a hotplate. But there is a small writing desk (that I bought and installed) and this wonderful balcony with this glorious view of the Central Valley. The view is to the east, and in the morning the sun rises over the distant hills, lighting up the vast valley that stretches beyond the red tile roofs of the few houses that my vista overlooks. The afternoon sun does not hit my windows, so my studio stays cool (a blessing in the heat because there's no AC), but the setting sun turns the distant hills various shades of yellow, orange, and sometimes red. And I often sit out on my balcony in the evening with a glass of Sangria and watch the hills change from yellow to orange to blue before they disappear into the blackness.

    There is still a timelessness to this place. I see it in the mothers walking their children to school each morning. In the afternoon the mothers walk back to the school and wait in a group for the school to let out, so they can walk their children back home. I see it in the farmers on Saturday mornings (if I'm up that early) guiding their mule-pulled wooden carts full of fruits or vegetables down to the Saturday open-air market in the local square. I hear it in the church bells of the large Catholic Church. They ring every thirty minutes around the clock, counting out the hours on the hour and then ringing one bell every half-hour. I like the timelessness of this place. It won't last, of course. Humanity is changing. Children back in the States are growing up without ever seeing stars in the pitch-black sky. They are given iPads instead of pacifiers. Their brains are being rewired—have already been rewired—and they are being transformed into the alien creatures that we always thought would arrive from outer space.

But... not my problem now. I'm too old. And besides, I came here to avoid Yeats's vision of the new world order slouching towards Bethlehem. And I have more or less succeeded.

The trick to survival, I always thought, is to dodge as many bullets as you can. You can't dodge them all, which is what life is all about, but the more you can dodge, the happier you will be. At least that's what I always thought, and that's what I have done.

And when I say bullets, I am talking of course about the aforementioned marriage, kids, debt, poverty, obligations, family, and stupidity. It takes brains to dodge marriage and kids. It takes money to dodge debt and poverty. It takes luck to dodge stupidity.

The bullets are invisible. They are infused into our culture. The guns are aimed at us from the moment we are born, and they start firing as soon as we need something that someone else has. The breast is withheld when we bite. We must learn to suck in a civilized way if we wish to survive. Growing up is running the gauntlet in a rifle range—everyone is shooting at you, making you move, dance, perform, and above all, making you run towards the future, towards *their* future, not yours. All bullets are invisible. Most people simply don't make it. They are picked off whenever the shooters grow tired of watching them crawl wounded on the ground. Most deaths are mercy killings.

But I digress... I was talking about Villa Rosario and gringos. Villa Rosario used to be better, but that's true of everyplace and everything. Hell, *I* used to be better. *You* used to be better. But nothing stays static—we are always devolving, always falling apart. The pretty young girls I knew in high school are unrecognizable today, as I'm sure I am to them (though not to myself). We layer over with fat, wrinkles, jowls, prejudices, conceits, impatience, and petty murderous jealousies.

I don't think anyone gets better with age. Once in a great while you meet a good person who has somehow managed to stay good during the course of their life—like my friend Carolina—but the rest of us... well shit, we get nastier and meaner and stupider. So one of the secrets of dodging bullets is to try to only hang out with those few other people who have managed to maintain their goodness... if you can find them. Be generous to them; be kind to them; do whatever it takes so that they will let you spend time with them. Which leads to the other secret of dodging bullets: avoiding the idiots. I don't mean being polite but distant. I don't mean being formal but courteous. I mean avoid them completely. Do not talk to them. Do not interact with them. They will slime all over you.

Take Lorenzo, for example. He's a gringo (of course). Came down here about three years ago from New York or New Jersey or NewFuckSomewhere. Thinks he's the Italian Stallion. A big fat fuck. Wears gold chains and white T-shirts. Plops himself down every day in one of the outdoor coffee shops near the plaza and sits there all day, waiting for anyone who speaks English to come along (because he won't take the time to learn Spanish) so he can grab them and hold them captive and spout his opinions about what a miserable third world shithole this town is. Everything out of his mouth is a complaint: how Immigration won't grant him residency (because of a few youthful indiscretions that led to criminal convictions); how the women only want him for his money; how the local restaurants try to overcharge him; how the electricity is unreliable; how the health care system here sucks... he can talk for days. I always keep an eye peeled for him. If I see him, I walk the other way. If I have to walk near the plaza and see him at that coffee shop, I will walk three blocks out of my way, around the entire plaza, to avoid him. I'm a better person for avoiding him. The extra few minutes of walking are well worth the reward of not having to deal with him. Because if he sees you, he will wave you over. And if you keep walking he will get up and approach you, and almost drag you back to his table "just for a minute" so that he can ejaculate his opinions all over you for the next thirty minutes. Bluntness or rudeness doesn't faze him a bit. You could say, "If you don't like it here, go home," and he will be happy you said that because he will use that as a talking point on how "if they only did X or Y or Z better here, it would be perfect." That's the thing about gringos—they have a fucking opinion about everything. You never meet a gringo down here (or in the United States either) who simply will say "I don't know" when you ask him a question about something he has no experience with. For example, you ask any gringo which is better, fusion or fission nuclear energy, and they will start out, "Well in my opinion..." and then commence to create an opinion on the spot, anything that mirrors some other opinion they have, even though they don't have a fuckounce of knowledge about nuclear energy. "Well, in my opinion, the best nuclear energy is the greenest, and from what I've read, fission produces less toxic waste, but of course, it would be better if we could harness the sun's energy..." or use our coal or use oil, or whatever dumbfuck opinion they have about energy and natural resources. Gringos always have opinions—about everything—and if they don't know something, they make up an opinion. It's a disease.

Of course... I'm a gringo too...

Despite what you may have assumed by my name, I am a US citizen. I grew up in the south. As a boy, I used to spend hours digging for Civil War musket balls in the red clay around the farm in Virginia where I was raised. I've been to Gettysburg, Appomattox,

Monticello, and the Vietnam Veterans Memorial Wall. I went to law school and practiced probate law for many years. If you had passed me in the courthouse—if you had noticed me at all—I would have looked like any other white guy in a suit. So, I'm qualified to talk about gringos—because I am one. And I'm able to talk about them, because I don't live in the US. It's only when you leave a place that you can see it for what it really is. Likewise, it's only when you leave another person that you can put the pieces together to figure out who that person really was.

But I digress. I was talking about Villa Rosario. It's hot here year around, almost a constant 85 degrees each afternoon. And humid. We have heavy rains from May through November, and when I say heavy, I'm talking monsoons... deluges. I like them. There are fewer gringos here in the rainy season. It's a good time to sit out on one's balcony and watch the thunderstorms roll across the central valley and sip on a Sangria.

Villa Rosario started getting popular with gringos a few years back, when La Chorrera's rents started to go up. For many years, La Chorrera was the go-to gringo enclave, because it was just outside of Panama City, but was safer and cheaper. Gringos needed a quiet place to sleep off the excesses of Panama City. That's the only reason gringos go to Panama City, you know... or Bangkok, or Vietnam, or Reno... for the excesses—the gambling and the whores. I'm not against gambling or prostitution, but sexual tourism attracts the worst gringos. I'm just stating the facts: Gringos do not come to Panama City for the pineapples. They come for the strip clubs, the casinos, and the whores. Anyway, Panama City started getting too excessive, too loud, and a bit too dangerous. And gringos discovered they could stay in La Chorrera where it was quiet and safe, but still be less than an hour away from the action in Panama

City. And La Chorrera responded by opening its own casinos and brothels, and a miniature Panama City was born, which of course attracted more gringos. Then, of course, La Chorrera started getting a bit too loud, a bit too dangerous, and the gringos started moving to Villa Rosario so they could sleep off the excesses of La Chorrera. We don't have any casinos and brothels yet (just a few hookers) but I'm sure they're coming. It's just a matter of time. Gringos ruin everything.

Mind you, there is nothing wrong with excess. We humans need excess. Every Eskimo needs his or her Eskimo Amok. Every Amish needs his or her Rumspringa. Every Jekyll needs his Hyde. But excess should be done with moderation, or at least discretion. Civilization works much better when people keep their excess on the down low. I remember visiting Amsterdam for the first time some thirty-five years ago... it was so easy to pick out the US kids—they were stoned and loud, so loud... yelling, bragging, swearing, and stumbling down the street, straight into the arms of the police... but the Dutch kids were all discretely stoned, very quiet. You never noticed them. It's the visible excess that always gets people in trouble. "Discreet excess"—that has always been my motto.

Anyway, back to Villa Rosario... we have two seasons here: the dry season and the wet season. The temperature remains the same. It's just a question of whether it rains or not. At this moment we are at the early months of the rainy season. The mornings are clear. The rains start around noon and continue late into the evening.

When I came to Villa Rosario, fifteen years ago, there were only a few other gringos here. There was no community of gringos—no support system—so to survive here, a gringo had to speak Spanish. Some married panameñas and were almost accepted by the locals. But no gringo is ever really "accepted" here—there's never a Tod Browning "one of us" moments. Gringos can find a way to fit in, more or less, be tolerated, maybe even liked... but we're always foreigners, *extranjeros* as they say in Spanish—"strangers". It's best to act like an *invitado*, a guest, someone who's been invited, someone who stays with permission... That's really all we are. The same way the Spaniards in Spain recently welcomed the refugees from Syria and Morocco. They welcomed them—as guests—because there's still that old memory in the back of their collective Spanish minds about having been conquered and ruled by the Moors for seven hundred years that keeps them from totally accepting the refugees. There's nothing like the memory of exploitation to keep you on guard. And Lord knows, the panameños here have their memories too. I'm amazed they don't murder us in our sleep.

But anyway, I'm an old man now, an old man in a wet month, who is thinking of one last trip to Europe, one last hurrah while I can still get around on my own... all on account of how my pee smelled this morning... Oh? You think that's a little crazy? You think your decisions are made more rationally? They are not. Our so-called rational free-will mind is just a tiny ice cube in a vast and deep unconscious sea. You think you know yourself? We spend half of our lives in a state of reality so bizarre that we are forced to purge it from our consciousness every morning the instant we wake up just so we can hang onto our fragile identity. What we call rationality is just a series of mental twitches that evolved in cavemen's brains to let them react when they heard a noise in the bushes. The basis of decision-making is fear and greed, not rationality. My intuition whispered that death is coming; I am afraid of death; I want to enjoy Europe again; I am greedy to enjoy those places where nothing encumbers... so my mind constructs a rational excuse to let me flee the thing I fear and move toward the experience I am greedy for. Rationality is just the method we humans use to create excuses we need to do the things we want. It's not wrong. After all, my pee said death is coming. Pee does not lie. So, why not go to Europe? Hopefully, it will be a glorious time and not my appointment in Samarra.

Oh... you're not familiar with the Samarra reference? Ah... I find it more and more true, the older I get, that the cultural references of my youth are no longer literary currency. Not that I'm convinced that people really communicate anyway, but it is nice when they have the same understanding of some phrase or reference. I used the expression "not worth a tinker's dam" the other day and the gringa I was talking to just stared at me. She assumed I meant "not worth a damn" which I guess was close enough, but still...

It's just further proof that things are devolving. I'm told that *Walden* is not taught as much in US schools anymore because the writing is considered too difficult for modern students—the long allegorical paragraphs with their complex sentence structure require too much effort... The problem is not the book. The problem is that thinking in the US has been replaced with reductionism. Everything has been reduced to something that can be Googled. If Thoreau was alive today, he would have written "Our life is Twittered away by detail."

But back to where I started. Is it beyond reason to think that certain scents can indicate underlying processes? You can tell an alcoholic from their body odor. Vegetarians can tell who eats meat by their scent. Dogs can be trained to detect cancer in humans from the faint scent that wafts from cancerous cells. Tibetan medicine men—who are trained doctors—still place a patient's urine in a bowl and whip it into a frothy mixture and sniff it as a diagnostic tool. I'm not saying I have cancer—I don't believe that. But I do believe that death is programmed into the genetic code in our bodies. We are programmed to die at a certain point. Every experienced hospital nurse knows that if you keep a patient artificially alive past "their time", that all the rest of the organs just start failing one by one. Why would it be unreasonable that a person could have a foreshadowing of their own death? By smell or intuition or deduction? Not as a morbid thing, but as a useful evolutionary skill that would allow us to make the best use of our time.

In the same way that birds disappear before earthquakes, I think we should take advantage of these intuitive moments. There has to be some scientific logic to intuition, just as there is a certain intuitive symmetry to good logic. Maybe death is near or maybe not. Maybe the gods want me in Europe for some reason or not. Or maybe it's just time to make an honest accounting of myself.

I think it's only the intimation of death that makes us take stock of ourselves. I remember a friend years ago who quit his job after he suffered a heart attack. He referred to his decision as "hearing the fluttering of angels' wings". It's the only thing that really stops us, that makes us think.

In the Carlos Castaneda books, don Juan Matus claimed death was an advisor—that death could speak to us. I don't know about that. It seems odd to me that death would take compassion on us, would offer us advice… maybe he meant that when we sense death is near, we advise ourselves. So maybe when my pee said that death is coming, I knew it was time for a reckoning, because I sensed a destiny, an end point, a final stepping-off place…

A stepping off place—that's what Jeduthan

Hawley called death in Edgar Lee Masters' *Spoon River Anthology*... Isn't it amazing that for all our science and knowledge, we simply do not know what death is? That undiscovered country from whose bourn no traveler returns—that what Shakespeare called it. The fact is, we simply don't know. We think that death is horrible because people look so horrible when they die. But wouldn't it be ironic if the entire human race was wrong about death? What if it was just like an orgasm? What if we make that same horrible face when we die like we do when we climax, when we squeeze our eyes shut and lose ourselves in some orgasmic universe that carries us far away in an infinite sea of pleasure? Wouldn't it be ironic if that's why we choose to come back, choose reincarnation—so that we can die again and experience that same pleasure? Except that we've forgotten that we chose to come back because that decision was made in the same dreamland as all our dreams. Maybe life is like going to the same crappy bar every night hoping to meet someone. Maybe life is one big blind date with death where you finally get lucky... I don't think it's true, but it would be ironic.

    Speaking of sex...

CHAPTER TWO: PLACES WHERE NOTHING ENCUMBERS

I remember Johnny Kaufman's upstairs bedroom. We were all in the sixth grade. Once or twice a week, four or five of us would meet at his house after school—his parents were at work—and we would go up to Johnny's room. He had copies of Playboy magazine that he had stolen from his father. We would look at the naked women with their huge tits. We would marvel at the beauty of these naked unattainable creatures, and then we would suck each other's cocks.

I have no idea where we got the idea to suck each other's cocks. We were all too young to actually cum. We didn't know what cumming was. But we were old enough to get erections, and it felt good to suck cock or to have your cock sucked.

I liked sucking Johnny's cock the best. It always tasted a bit like soap. Maybe he washed himself before we came over—I don't know.

But upstairs in Johnny's locked bedroom, well, that was all I got in the way of sex education. Until sometime in the seventh grade when an older boy named Mike Dimaggio told us that if we stroked our cocks long enough, white liquid would shoot out of the tip.

I tried it one time in my bathroom at home alone. When I came, I swear, I saw colored sparkles, like a thousand little stars in my cum. I had never felt like that before. I was amazed! Amazed and scared. I thought I had broken my cock. I had no idea what the purpose of this wizardry was, but once I figured out that I had not broken my cock, I jerked off as often as I could. I was clearly on my way to a lifetime of interest in sex.

I don't remember when I figured out that that what we boys were doing was not permitted, not allowed. I never heard the word "gay" or "faggot" back then. But somehow—again in seventh grade—I pieced together that what I was doing was not approved of, and that in fact I could get into trouble—into very great trouble—if anyone else found out. And so, I withdrew from that group of boys. When eighth grade rolled around, we all went off to different schools anyway, and I never saw them again.

What I do remember, and what I think I carried forward with me for my entire life, was a type of modus operandi about "feeling safe in a place," that is, feeling safe enough for sex. There was something about Johnny's bedroom that was safe. His parents were not coming home. We were alone in the house. None of us were going to tell anyone what we did. The Playboys were there; the women were naked; so clearly, the gods were giving their blessings that we could do whatever we wanted. There was a sense that we were not going to be discovered, so we were free to be ourselves, as it were... maybe that's the origin of being "in the closet"... being in a dark place where you can have sex without being discovered.

I feel the same way now about gay bathhouses. They exist all over the world and they are uniformly safe and discrete. Very discrete. Their entrances are unmarked. Any citizen walking by would have no idea what lay behind those doors.

    I don't think that my perception of safe places is personal. Rather, I think it is universal, because every bathhouse in the world has exactly the same set-up, the same set of rules, the same polite behaviors by its patrons, and almost the same physical layout. The front door is unmarked. You find out the location on the internet, in gay publications, or by word of mouth in the gay community. Somehow you find your way there. You walk in. There is a short hallway that leads to a cashier's window where you pay your admission fee. The light in the hallway is dim, so that if there is a line waiting to pay, you have the excuse of not recognizing anyone. You pay and go in. Inside there is a counter where you are handed a towel, and a pair of flip-flops or plastic sandals, and a key—to either a locker or a room—depending on which you paid for. The locker room is right there, and you find your locker, or you go down another hallway and find your room. The light inside the bathhouse is even dimmer, and sometimes you have to wait until your eyes adjust so that you can read the room numbers on the doors. In any event, whether at your locker or inside your room, you remove your clothes, wrap your towel around you, and head to the showers.

    The showers are always one large room, where you shower naked with other men. There is plenty of liquid soap in the containers on the wall. There is always an emphasis on being clean in the bathhouses. And harkening back to Johnny's soapy cock, I appreciate that. Everyone at the bathhouse washes their bodies, their faces, their underarms, their cocks, and their asses. Sometimes there is some eye contact that occurs in the showers, which leads to some touching. It's not uncommon to see men washing each other, soaping up each other's cocks just for the simple pleasure of doing so.

Such a strange thing, don't you think? That three minutes after entering an establishment, that you could be standing naked with a total stranger, both lovingly soaping each other's cocks? How is such a thing possible? How is such permission granted? It's because of the place—it's a place where nothing encumbers. It's also a place where there is no talking required.

And further down the hallways there are various rooms: steam rooms, dry heat rooms, dark rooms, play rooms, rooms with porno, rooms with slings and tie-down beds, and rooms that are completely black for totally anonymous sex. Again, no talking is required.

Not that all bathhouses are gay. There are many sex clubs with the same set-up, and there are many gay bathhouses that are open to men and women on certain days. And the exact same thing happens. And it's all with the most respectful and polite consent. A woman will position herself on one of the many couches in one of the playrooms and raise her head and make eye contact with men, and the men will quietly line up, and patiently wait their turn, and she will blow as many of them as she wants. Are you surprised? There are women in this world, my friend, who love giving blow jobs just as much as gay men do. I remember watching one woman blow twenty guys in a row, taking their cum, swallowing it, and going on to the next one, until she got tired, and then simply stood up and went to her room to rest.

Many male-female couples come to the bathhouses on "co-ed" nights. Some couples are exhibitionists and only fuck each other, but like to do it while others watch; others are couples where the man is a cuckold, and enjoys watching his woman have sex with other men before he fucks her; and then there are those couples consisting of bisexual partners where the man and the woman will both sit on the couch and both suck off as many men as possible... the variety is endless... and there are some lesbian women who come to the bathhouses looking for other lesbians too... not as many, but occasionally.

But the point I'm trying to make is more about the place than the sex... Places exist that give permission, that let a person be closer to their true selves. People need places like that... well, people like me anyway.

And it's the places that we carry in our memories that motivate us. We try and recreate them everywhere we go, like Dorothy trying to get back to Auntie Em's farm to Kansas; those memories of home, even temporary spaces like bathhouses that become home to our desires, that form our identity, that we carry for decades, that compel us to search out similar places to recreate those same personal experiences. No wonder the Hindus and the Buddhists believe in reincarnation. We reincarnate our secret places every chance we get. We have no choice... at least, that's the way I've always experienced it.

What else but reincarnation explains why, no matter where I travel, I have sought out those places? If some job sent me to some city for some training, I would prepare myself by researching what bathhouses, sex clubs, gay bars, and swingers' clubs might exist in that city. Or if I thought about a vacation somewhere, I would do the same thing. It would be my quest—to find out if there was some place that would reincarnate the safe place. And ultimately, it really didn't matter if I had sex there or not. I would estimate that at least half of the times I have ever been in a gay bathhouse, I did not have sex with anyone—at least not sex to completion, as they say—because I couldn't find the right partner who appealed to me... but it didn't matter. It was sufficient to be in that place, with those naked people, all of us doing the same thing, all of us believing in the same force and following the same rules, all of us feeling relaxed that we were in a place where had the anonymity to be ourselves, our anonymous secret sensual selves.

The only times I was prevented from those activities was when I went on trips with one of my wives. Oh... you didn't know I had been married? Yes, twice in fact. For a total of almost nineteen years. And in both situations, it was—for a time—also a place of safety... but only for a time. That was my fault. I should have been more honest about who I was and what I wanted. But, as you may have guessed, I am not an honest person. Hence the need for secret places. My reincarnation occurs on the lower bardos, I guess. Maybe there are better sex clubs at the higher bardos, the higher levels of reincarnation, or maybe they have found something better than sex. I haven't. And so, no matter where I go: New York, Chicago, Denver, Los Angeles, London, Paris, Amsterdam, Barcelona, Lisbon... I seek out those places where nothing encumbers.

Now, I know what you're thinking. You're wondering how that makes me any different than the sexual tourist gringos who have ruined Panama City and La Chorrera, and who are now overrunning Villa Rosario. Well... I try to be discrete. If I am giving a reckoning of my life, I would have to admit that is the only difference—that I keep my wanderlust very quiet, very hidden. But I would add that discretion makes a cavernous difference. I'm not getting drunk in some

Bangkok bar talking in loud terms about going to fuck some ladyboy; I'm not offering some legitimate masseuse in Denver one hundred dollars for a "happy ending"; I'm not giving the bellboy ten dollars in Vietnam to bring a woman—any woman—up to my room; I'm not trying to negotiate down some dirt-poor rentboy on a side street in Madrid from fifty Euros down to thirty; I'm not circling the zócalo in some Mexican town in my big rental car looking for streetwalkers. In short, I am not visible. If I travel somewhere new, I buy a regular guidebook, I see the sights, I have a nice dinner, and then maybe I'll slip away in a cab to a certain address, go inside, and then emerge a few hours later and take a cab back to the hotel. Very quiet, very discrete.

    I remember one sex club slash bathhouse that I visited in Frankfurt, Germany, years ago. I was sitting in a tiny steam room with several other men. We were all just taking in the steam, sitting naked on our towels (because the tiles were hot) when a couple came into the room. The man removed his towel and placed it on the ledge but did not sit down. The woman removed her towel but then turned around, her back to her man, to face us men who were all sitting down in front of her watching. Her man started playing with her ass. Those of us sitting and watching did not move. The woman's man got hard and he inserted his cock into her from behind, still standing. Finally, the man said, "You can touch her" to all of us who were sitting down, and we all stood up and moved towards them. We all gently touched her breasts, stroked her hair, touched her shoulders, and her torso as this guy was fucking her from behind. I reached down and felt her pussy and felt this guy's cock going in and out. The only sound was the sound of the steam hissing in the steam room. It was all so quiet, so gentle, and—dare I say it?—so natural. The couple started getting more excited, and the man sat down on his towel on the ledge and the woman sat on top of him, and they fucked for a few minutes more and then she reached behind and gently tapped him, and they got up and left.

Now compare that to any hotel bar in the Cangrejo section of Panama City. There will always be a table of loud gringos, and the hookers will be rotating through the room, walking by their table, trying to make eye contact, "presenting themselves" as they say, while the men make loud and degrading remarks. "Did you see the tits on that one?" is probably the most common question uttered in a Panama bar. But those poor girls are just trying to make a living. Almost all of them have babies at home—often babies *and* parents to support—and those gringos will drink and banter and harass and haggle price with those poor hookers until some deal is cut. Compare those two scenes. Both are about sex, but only one is discrete and respectful.

Now, I will be the first to admit that I could be wrong. There may be no difference between me and those obnoxious entitled gringos at the bar in Panama City. I'd like to think there is, but... I am aware, as Freud said, that denial is the strongest psychological defense. But I'm just trying to lay out my beliefs—which are that sexual excess is necessary, and that discretion and politeness are the only ingredients that allow all the parties to partake in that excess safely and without losing their humanity.

But excess is a relative term... or perhaps I should say that excess is a personal term. One's man's mild excess is another man's deepest abhorrence... so maybe it's the place after all—maybe it's the place that is the only constant. Maybe it's our need for some type of sanctuary... do you know what I mean? Maybe we need that place more than we need what happens in that place, the same way the suburban husband goes out to his garage for hours on the weekend, just to tinker...

But, speaking for me, I need both. I need the sex to take my mind off the horror of death, but I won't do the sex if I don't feel safe. I have to feel safe.

But safety is always just a temporary feeling...

CHAPTER THREE: THE RECKONING

Thoreau didn't actually use the word "reckoning". What he actually said was, "Moreover, I, on my side, require of every writer, first or last, a simple and sincere account of his own life..." But I think he was letting himself—and everyone else—off too easy here. To give a "simple account" of one's life, a modest summation, *is* the first step, but an account without self-reflection is just a story. After any simple account, the questions always arise: What does it mean? What was the point? You spend three-fourths of a century on this planet, for what end?

Horace Mann said, "Be ashamed to die until you have won some victory for humanity." And I know why he said it that way—he was trying to exhort students to social activism. And if you can do that—great. But I'm not talking about social activism; I'm talking about self-awareness and meaning. And in that regard, I would be happy with some small victory for my own humanity.

So anyway, I like the word "reckoning" because it means more than just the act of story-telling. A reckoning is the settlement of the account; the totaling of the entire bill and a contemplation of what was spent, what was gained, and what was lost; a summation of one's life and a reflection of its value. And to me, most importantly, it does not involve a judgment.

Preachers love to threaten that "on the day of

judgment we will be held accountable." And, of course, they claim that the good will be rewarded, and the bad (which is everyone they don't like) will be damned to burn in hell.

But *judgment* is a horrible word... and always leads to a *verdict* and *condemnation*... terms that don't tend to lead to self-improvement in the psychological sense. As soon as you judge somebody—or yourself—you have condemned them, and no further change is possible—no change in your relationship as the judge over that person and no change in yourself. But a reckoning is different. Because what is the point of self-reflection if not to change oneself? "Why show me this, if I am past all hope?" Scrooge begged the Spirit of the Future in the cemetery when Scrooge was forced to view his own grave.

So I guess that's what I'm doing—providing my own ghostly visitors. It does seem that one first has to provide a summation, and then that summation becomes a reckoning, the same way a pile of organic matter becomes compost... dust to dust, as the preachers also like to point out.

And here's the important part: If it wasn't for death, there would be no reckoning. In fact, there would be no consciousness, no discernment. It's only death that makes us wonder what the fuck we did with our lives.

I remember the first dead person I ever saw. I was sixteen years old, working as a volunteer aide in the x-ray department of a small general hospital. They needed the portable x-ray machine moved down to the morgue one night, and I got the job. The reason they needed it, it turned out, was that a young woman had committed suicide, or so the police thought, by shooting herself in the head with a gun. Women don't usually use guns to kill themselves, and so the police wanted an x-ray to examine the trajectory of the bullet to see if it was consistent with a self-inflicted wound. It was. But the coroner, unmindful of my young age, gestured me into the examining room to show me the body.

"Here," he said, pointing to the hole in the front of the woman's head, "here you can see how this hole is smaller and this hole in the back is larger..." He stuck his finger in the larger hole to show me the difference in size. "This is where the bullet went in, and this is where it came out." Her face, caked with dried blood, mouth agape, was as cold and gray as the steel table she was lying on, but I could tell she was in her twenties. I said nothing. I think the image of him sticking his finger deep inside the hole of that poor woman's head will stay with me all my life.

The cop, who was standing beside me, added, "Yeah, a lot of people think shooting yourself in the head is a fast way to die, but it isn't. Your body flops around for a long time. There was blood all over this girl's floor and ceiling from where she was flopping around."

I suppose they were trying to educate me. In a way, they did. I'll say it again: There is nothing like death to make you wonder about life.

I have seen many more dead bodies since then, of course. Most men have, one way or another. I don't know if most women have. I suspect not.

And maybe death is just a metaphor for living responsibility. After all, it's not death, the physical end... it's the fact that there will be no more time left, no more chances, no more opportunities to improve, to do *something*—whatever that something is—to do something with one's life. It's the fact that life ends, just ends, and one... as Allen Ginsberg wrote in his poem "Flash Back"... one just *isn't here* anymore.

It's funny isn't it? That the same thing—death—that causes us to wonder about the point of life... also causes us to pursue debauchery. I, who am sitting here writing this now, a mere twenty-four hours ago, was at the gay bathhouse fucking men in the ass. I think I fucked about four of them. With a condom of course. And not to orgasm. It was in a darkroom, and the place was packed. About six fellows were up on these padded benches that lined the darkroom; they were on their knees, their asses sticking out to the center of the room, and various men would take turns sticking their cocks into these offered asses. I took my turn too. I have to say, I'm not sure why. I don't really like being a top. Truth be told, there's not a lot of physical pleasure in fucking a stranger in the ass. After all, the only contact to the cock is with the sphincter muscles—and, yes, they are tight—but the rest of the rectum doesn't offer much contact, does it? I think the pleasure from being a top derives more from dominating someone. I guess. Like I say, I don't really get off on it. Yet, I did it, to several fellows last night, because after all, I was in the bathhouse and it was dark, and I was horny I guess, and I wanted to try it and so I tried it several times... but all in all, looking back on it today, I could have skipped it. So here you go—in the same few pages I have gone from describing death—the ultimate horror—and the motivation to take stock of one's life and *do something* and then in the same pages described fucking some men from behind while I reached around and fondled their dicks. Can this be reconciled? How? How is it that debauchery and divinity spring from the same awareness of death? From the same motivation?

Well, here's another piece of the puzzle: I didn't plan on going to the bathhouse last night. I just ended up there because I had nothing better to do. When debauchery is available, it becomes the something better to do. I wasn't even that horny. But I was a bit lonely. And so... I ended up there. Looking for love? I hate to be that cliché, but really, isn't that what we're all doing? Well, I'll get back to that in a minute. But anyway, I was at the bathhouse last night, enjoying my debauchery, more or less, or maybe I was just killing time with debauchery because nothing better was coming along, and at some point, I had had enough, and I just wanted to cum and go home. I had been there for maybe two hours, and had some nice young man suck my cock while he sniffed poppers, and then I fucked him (with a condom of course) for a bit, and then I fucked those three or four other guys in the aforementioned darkroom, and then I watched some porn in the porn room, and then I wandered through all the corridors of the darkroom a bit and felt up a bunch of cocks and then, as I said, I thought I'd like to cum and go home... But there I was, standing against the wall in the darkroom (which as the name implies is really dark) trying to find someone to touch, but everyone was occupied, a room full of maybe twenty guys, fucking, sucking and stroking, and there I was masturbating myself to orgasm because I couldn't find someone to touch... Now, isn't that the ultimate loneliness, masturbating yourself to orgasm by yourself in a room full of men fucking/sucking each other? It's like the ending of the porn movie *The Devil In Miss Jones* —which is actually a really great pornified version of *Les Jeux Sont Fait*— where this girl is given a chance to return to earth after she dies to experience sex but ends up back in eternity stuck in a room with a man who can't get it up. But that's how I felt last night, having rubbed my dick raw in a pointless pursuit of debauchery because I had nothing better to do in this world... I mean, think about it. Oh wait, you think you're that different? Ah my friend, I beg to differ. You are the same as me.

And when I say "you", I am referring to those of you, if any, reading this now and understanding it. I am not referring to general humanity. I have walked amongst the masses and am amazed at what passes for humanity. I am amazed more by the individual being that passes in front of me in the street than by any Taj Mahal or any Great Pyramid or Stonehenge. In fact, these human creatures share many attributes with their famous monuments: they are both incomprehensible, hidden in mystery, and ultimately pointless. Among the seven wonders of the world are not included the Great Slugs, and yet what else do you call these highly evolved pointless bodies of protoplasm?

Well, maybe I am being too harsh... It's just that I cannot really stand being around people... Well no, that's not true... the way I actually experience it is that people prefer not to be around me. Language is important. If you describe a thing wrong, people assume that your description is the thing itself.

Anyway, the point is, I submit to you, dear Reader, that you are not that different than me. That does not relieve me of my obligation to provide a reckoning of my life—it's just an observation. You have your sixth-grade sexual experiences, your debaucheries, your desires, and your horrors too... don't you?

CHAPTER FOUR: RELATIONSHIPS

I was Skyping with Carolina the other day and she asked me: "How do you know if someone is a good person, and more importantly, how do you relate that information to yourself?" And it took me a minute to realize what she was driving at. My first impression was that she was just asking how do you know if someone you've met is a decent human being. After all, the context of our conversation was the fact that she had just broken up with her boyfriend who, after two years of living together, turned out to be a rather immature jerk. "Turned out to be" is the wrong expression, for he had been that way all along, and she had seen signs of that all along, and yet she had moved in with him anyway.

But then I realized that she was asking something quite different—that the second part of her question, the "how do you relate that information to yourself?" was describing the most subtle and difficult part of the relationship equation. For who among us has not spent time... or shared a bed... with someone who we *knew* was not a great match for us, but who for that moment was *good enough*? That's the problem, isn't it? We meet someone and we are lonely, so we accept an invitation to have a beer, to have dinner, to share a bed... It's like that old quip about a guy who might not be Mr. Right, but he's Mr. Right Now.

And so it unfolded for Carolina, as it unfolds for all of us throughout our lives. She met someone who shared some interests with her... he met about 50% of whatever internal criteria she has. They enjoyed hiking together. They both had evenings free. Then of course, sex reared its head. And let's face it, it's tough to find an acceptable sex partner. I'm not talking a great sex partner—I mean, it's tough just to find someone acceptable enough to have sex with... someone whose hygiene and skill level are adequate enough. Shit—sometimes we even lower those standards if we're horny or lonely enough. I remember one bathhouse in Spain where I encountered a short fat balding bear of a man in one of the dark corridors. He paused and gently ran his hand over my chest.

And so it unfolded for me, as it unfolds for all of us throughout our lives, that I let him take my hand and guide me into one of the little rooms with a bed and close the door behind us.

Now you could say that it was just horniness that made me to that. But there's more to it, and it relates to Carolina's question. Because in that moment with that man, in the first few seconds of our encounter in the dark hallway, when he ran his fingers over my chest, there was terabyte of information being imparted back and forth, and in that touch, I *knew* I could trust him, at least enough to step into a small sex room with him. So, the information is always there, at least enough information for the next few minutes.

They say that when insects attack a plant, the plant sends out a warning to all the nearby plants through thread-like filaments of fungi that connect their roots to their neighbors' roots. That's not enough information for the nearby plants to plan far into the future, but it's enough for the immediate moment.

Maybe relationship information works the same way. Maybe it's like those electronic signs at the bus stations in Spain that tell you how many minutes until the next bus, and which bus number is coming next. The signs don't tell you the schedule for the next hour or the next day or the rest of your life—they just give you enough information so you can decide whether to sit and wait two more minutes or whether you have time to go across the street and get a cup of coffee. Maybe the signs we receive from the other person are just that limited—just enough information for the next decision.

Like a game of poker, everyone wants to see each other's hand... but all we get are "tells"—little microbursts of information—and that's where our intuition has to do its wonderful mysterious work. And it's really all happening at the subconscious level isn't it? All relationships are chemical—and everything that happens between two humans unfolds at that level, out of our control. Everything initially, at any rate. But at some point, the other player has to put their cards down. At some point early in a relationship, the other person will show you their full hand, will give you enough information that suddenly—intuitively and accurately—you know what kind of player you are dealing with.

Maya Angelo wrote: "Believe a person the first time they show you who they are." That is so true. But I would alter it to say: "Believe yourself and your intuition the first time a person shows you who they are."

Nature is as good at revealing as it is at camouflaging. The other person *will* show you their hand—those are the rules of the game—and then they will quickly remix the cards and deal another closely guarded hand. But in that split second of their first reveal—before they mix the cards up—that is the moment when you can know what kind of person you are dealing with—whether he or she is kind, intelligent, fair, hardworking, etc., or whether they are just another player out to fleece you.

But you don't have to wait until the other person shows their hand. To continue my poker metaphor, I think it's possible to *call* another person's hand, to make them show you their cards early in the relationship. How? Well, it's tough to explain exactly. But don Juan Matus believed that it was possible to *see* another person—to look at them in a way—in a way where you open up your own intuition—and you can, in essence, see through their cards, see the cards they are holding. All the information is already there, like the way that swarthy man in the bathhouse touched me gently... if you're sitting at the bar and the guy next to you gestures for the waitress in a dismissive, condescending way—that's more than just a *tell*, that's his whole hand of cards.

One of the reasons I am musing on these matters is that I had met Carolina's now ex-boyfriend early in their relationship, and I could tell he was a jerk. Not a total jerk. He was a good-time kinda guy, a "let's get a beer" kinda guy, smart enough to work the system so he didn't have to work that hard, but not bright enough to really think about life much further than tonight's choice of bars. He was a talker, full of stories, friendly, and charming in a laid-back way. But I wondered what she saw in him. Well, she told me later that he was good at sex. Men who are good at sex, especially if they are decent looking, can be very dangerous to women, because women rarely find men who are good at sex, and so they will overlook immaturity and selfishness. Eventually, of course, being only good at sex is not enough to sustain a relationship. Those relationships usually crash and burn after about two years. I don't know why two years is the norm. I don't make the rules; I just observe them.

Since I have opened Pandora's Box on the topic of relationships, I should talk about love... but since this is supposed to be an honest reckoning, I have to admit that I know nothing about love and thus have nothing to say about it.

I know that I must have believed that I was "in love" at several points in my life—after all, I married twice—but I cannot remember what it felt like, and by that I mean that I cannot remember the actual sensation of love, the physical feeling. I do remember, years ago, reading George Bernard Shaw's *Don Juan in Hell* where Don Juan (a very different Don Juan than don Juan Matus) was describing how powerless he was to resist a woman's charm, that even when he did not want to have sex with them, he could not resist the urge. He said, "But while I was in the act of framing my excuse to the lady, life seized me and threw me into her arms, as a sailor throws a scrap of fish into the mouth of a seagull." And I remember thinking how true that was for me. But of course, that is not love. It demeans it by calling it "just sex" as if sex were some annoying hunger pang between the more important meals of life. Sex *is* life—ask any biologist. What's love got to do with it?

Maybe that's how it is for women too, and maybe that's how it was for Carolina—that she was just about to tell that guy that they were not compatible when the life force picked her up and threw her into his arms. And why would the life force be so short-sighted? Maybe because it knows something that we humans refuse to accept—that life is short, that death is near, and that Mr. Right-Now may be Mr. Right-Before-I-Die. Maybe those electronic bus signs in Spain are truly like life—that life only tells you when the next bus arrives because that may be the last bus, and the life force figures that taking a bus ride somewhere is better than dying of a heart attack alone at the bus stop.

But sometimes we have to fight the life force. Not all love is good. Sometimes it's better to sit alone on the bench at the bus stop rather than take a ride that you don't know where it's going to end.

But as I say, I don't have anything to say about love because I don't know anything about it. I think love is like free will. Both are just out of reach.

CHAPTER FIVE: LOSING MY TRAIN OF THOUGHT

I often lose my train of thought. Sometimes it worries me because my mother had Alzheimer's and her father had dementia... although my uncle (my mother's brother) was sharp as a tack until he died at ninety-one, and my dad's side had no mental issues... but still I worry... because as I said, I often lose my train of thought. Part of that I blame on drinking, of course. The rest I blame on my being generally stupid.

I have written elsewhere about my epiphany... the day I realized that I was an idiot. Like Homer Clapp in Edgar Lee Masters' *Spoon River Anthology*, I awoke one day and realized that I was one of life's fools... and that there was no point in resisting it. I simply had to accept it. As I often tell Carolina, I am retarded. She hates it when I use that word, so occasionally I substitute the word "idiot", but idiot does not have the same meaning. We say the word "idiot" all the time: "So-and-so is just an idiot," which means we do not like him; or "I forgot the keys, like an idiot." But the word *retarded* a a comparison with the rest of the teeming masses. If you are retarded, you are held back, slower, left behind, stupider-than-them. The word compares you to other people. And ladies and gentlemen, I am retarded. I am not an idiot. I'm actually pretty smart. I did go to law school, after all. But I am retarded. I just don't fit in—

anywhere. But I am smart enough to hide it. That's the politician's trick, you know, being smart enough to hide the fact that you're retarded. I keep my mouth shut, and never, ever depend on other people.

The fact is, even as retarded as I am, I see things.

I remember, as a young man, finally realizing that some people were like onions—layer after layer with no center. It's not that they weren't human beings; it was just that they didn't have a center—you could never connect to anything real no matter how much time you spent with them. In fact, the more time you spent with them, the more they just showed you layer after layer... but no center. And it seems to me, as I have aged, that there are more and more of these onion people. I run into them all the time. Some days, they are the only ones you meet!

Yet, at the same time, I see that loneliness is the biggest problem facing everyone today. (In one recent study, 100% of people said they were lonelier now than they ever had been in their lives. I know this because I commissioned and organized and carried out the survey. But I ran short of funds, so I had to extrapolate the findings. But I stand by these findings.) And this rise in loneliness helps explain the increase in social media addiction and people being glued to their cell phones. In the same way I use anonymous sex in the bathhouse to substitute for love, the masses of people use electronic connections to substitute for real contact. It's a crappy substitute (on both counts), but you gotta do what you gotta do.

And maybe substitutes are the best I can do. It's been more than six or seven years since I was in a "relationship", meaning, dating someone, and that was Magali, a sweet prostitute here in Villa Rosario. Despite what you may think from her occupation, she was the sweetest woman I've ever known... but of course, she had her issues, which is why our relationship didn't last.

Maybe I've simply devolved since then. Maybe I aged out of the dating market. Maybe I'm retarded. Maybe early Alzheimer's has set in, and everyone is simply too kind to tell me. I don't know. But I haven't been able to sustain a relationship since Magali and I split up. I have tried, but I can't even get a date. Carolina says I'm still good looking, and I should try and date, but then... she is very kind.

The fact is, all of my sexual contact with women for the past six or seven years has been with prostitutes. Thank God for prostitutes. I would have put a bullet through my own brain if not for them.

But I digress. Where I was going was saying that on one hand some people are without a center, like John Prine's song *Some Humans Ain't Human*, yet at the same time, there's more and more loneliness, which must affect the onion people too. Are these two things related? Does the increase in onion people "cause" the increase in loneliness because there are fewer real people to connect to? Or does the increase in loneliness create more onion people?

Or... is anyone real? Is the best we can do is to get within the inner ring of one of the onion people? Is that why we're so lonely? Because there really is no one to connect to? Chris Rock claims that there are no soulmates—that the best you get in life is just a mate. I don't know. I do remember there were times in both my marriages when I was happy, when I had found someone who "fit". But of course, that feeling didn't last. Carolina says that all relationships have an expiration date. I hate to believe that, but it certainly has been my experience. We drift like satellites in a cold void and then for a while we travel in parallel arcs with some other nomadic satellite, and we enjoy their light as we burn through space together for a while, but then we watch as the gravity of their parabola pulls them away from us. And how do we explain the gravity of their arc to our friends but to say "they had issues"?

Is evolution just fucking cruel or what? In order to create these magnificent brains, we have to gestate for nine months and then spend twenty years just growing bigger and then spend another twenty years figuring shit out. The first decade of our lives is spent in almost total dependency while we imprint everything around us. No wonder we all crave love! No wonder we all crave someone to take care of us, to watch over us, to be our soulmate, to fulfill us—what other experience do we know? Take a mother away from a baby chimp, and the baby will cling to any warm piece of cloth. We talk about addiction as if it is something foreign to our nature—it *is* our nature. We are designed to need.

In another million years, when nature will have disposed of the human being experiment, it would be interesting to see what creature replaces us as the dominant species. Will some remnant of emotion, of love, of dependency still exist? Or will nature have tossed us, and our frail feelings, on the rubbish bin as another failed evolutionary experiment like the dodo, the quagga, the dinosaur, and the woolly mammoth?

But I digress... You see, that's what worries me. I was wanting to provide some context for my aloneness, my separateness from others; I was wanting to examine why I have given up on relationships with women, even after two marriages, and only find female contact with prostitutes. And yet I went off on some tangent about dinosaurs... well, I suppose maybe I'm a dinosaur of sorts... on my way to being extinct. After all, I have no children. I am the end of the line for my family. You can't get any more extinct than that.

Magali was not the first prostitute I lived with. Decades ago, between my first two marriages, back in the States, long before I moved to Villa Rosario, I lived with Amber. She worked as a "dancer" in what used to be called B-girl joint. She would dance topless and then get paid by the bar for encouraging patrons to buy drinks. That's where I met her. We hit it off and soon were living together. We were together for maybe six months before we broke up.

Amber was horribly dyslexic. Couldn't manage any kind of school. Dancing was one of the few options open to her. But she had a wicked sense of humor and a good understanding of her situation. She always said that her best bet would be to find some older rich guy to marry. Maybe that's why she hooked up with me—I don't know.

A lot of gringos think that all prostitutes are victims of trafficking. That's not true. What is true is that all of us are victims of life. Amber was a victim of being born poor and having her brain wired up wrong. But she was fiercely independent and nobody's fool.

I didn't mind it when she started turning tricks for extra money. She was careful and always used condoms. She would come home and shower and then regale me with stories of her clients, and then we would make love. It just didn't bother me.

But then she got into drugs... and that was a problem. My own experience with drugs—decades earlier—had almost killed me, and so I was adamantly against them. She thought she could handle them. Everyone thinks they can handle them. But I have certain limits, and drugs is one of them. We split up and lost touch with each other.

I read her obituary about a year later. She had died of an overdose. I looked up some her dancer friends and asked if it was an accidental overdose or suicide. None of them knew.

What is true about people like Amber, and people like Carolina's ex-boyfriend, is that you cannot save anyone. You can love them; you can ease the pain of their lives for a while... but you cannot save them. They are all satellites drifting in their own orbits, doomed to make the same circle through cold space until they burn out.

In fact... we barely have a chance at saving ourselves. As I mentioned, one day, decades ago, I had this epiphany—that I was an idiot, and that there was nothing I could do to change that. This was the key part of my epiphany—that there was nothing I could do to change my nature. I looked the way I looked; I worked as hard as my work ethic required; I thought the thoughts I thought; and I reacted to things the way I reacted. It was out of my control. No matter how I dressed or changed my hair for example, certain women (or men) were going to be attracted to me or not. No matter how hard I worked, I was either going to be selected for that certain job or not. No matter how I tried to control my behavior, people were going to see me the way they saw me and either like me or not. It was all simply out of my control. And so, I might as well give up any hope of achieving success through my own efforts and simply be myself and see what the gods had in store for me.

I was not the first person on earth to have this epiphany. Check out Ecclesiastes 9:11.

> *I returned, and saw under the sun, that the race is not to the swift, nor the battle to the strong, neither yet bread to the wise, nor yet riches to men of understanding, nor yet favor to men of skill; but time and chance happeneth to them all.*

And so, I gave up trying. And my life has been immeasurably happier since that day.

But it's not enough simply to know that you're an idiot. Even the most rural Oklahoma dumbfuck occasionally realizes he's not that bright. You have to go beyond that and realize that you are a dumbfuck who is *going to die*, and that you're going to die sooner than later.

Buddha said it best two thousand five-hundred years ago when he set forth the five pillars of Buddhism:

> *I am impermanent and subject to disease. I am impermanent and subject to decay. I am impermanent and subject to death. I will lose all that I love. I will inherit the consequences of my actions.*

I have fought off my infirmities (so far)... but I have aged and decayed... and my aloneness and my loneliness are the consequences I have inherited from my actions (and inactions)... and I have certainly lost all whom I have loved... so the only thing missing for me in Buddha's prophesy is being subject to death—which brings us full circle to the first chapter, my intimation of death in that waft of urine smell this morning. Was that only a few hours ago? Odd how memory bends time.

CHAPTER SIX: CIRCLES

But why even bother with a reckoning if there's no free will? Let me explain: When I was in fourth grade, I was in love with a girl named Margaret Papadopoulis. She was Greek. What I liked about her was her dark thick black hair and her tiny moustache. None of the girls in my fourth-grade class had hair as black as Margaret Papadopoulis. I was transfixed. And that faint moustache mesmerized me. I know that sounds odd but remember we're talking fourth grade here. There was this other girl named Sherry something-or-other, and I think she liked me because she would wet herself when we talked, but it was Margaret Papadopoulis that my heart was set on.

Margaret Papadopoulis lived near me, down a dead-end street that had a creek running nearby. I could walk to her house by following the creek, and that was the stealth route, because even back then, I did not want my desires to be known. I befriended her brother and showed him how to hunt for crayfish in the creek. That way I had an excuse to go by her house, and to be in the creek near her house.

I had no idea what I wanted. I just knew that I was attracted to her and wanted to be around her. I would walk up the creek by her house, pretending to look for crayfish, in the hopes that she might be outside, and I could "happen" to emerge from the creek from hunting crawfish and "happen" to chat with her. That never happened, of course. I spent countless afternoons getting my sneakers wet in the creek hoping for a chance to spot her. I never did.

You would think that school would have been the better place to strike up a conversation with a girl you were interested in, but in actuality, fourth grade is a highly regimented environment, with assigned seating, no talking, forming lines, and something about trying to learn in a classroom. I never got a chance to talk with her at school. Midway through the year, her family moved back to Greece, and I never saw her again.

The point of my telling you all this is to explain that that relationship set the pattern for all my relationships with women. That pattern was imprinted on my brain. I would become totally infatuated with someone for no reason at all. I would stealthily try and position myself so that I could happen to strike up a conversation with them. That hoped-for conversation would never occur. They would disappear. I repeated that pattern time after time in my life. I might meet women; I might talk with them; sometimes I might sleep with them; sometimes I might marry them; but the basic pattern was still the same. I never really knew them and eventually they disappeared.

And so my question to all you latent philosophers is this: If all our early patterns are imprinted on our brain; and we have no choice but to repeat them over and over (after all, Freud's definition of neurosis was simply the act of repeating unproductive behaviors); and if we have no actual choice in all this, what is the point of providing a reckoning about it? Or to put it in Christian terms: how can I be held accountable for behavior over which I have no real control? As the retard that I am, I embrace the fact that I have no control over my destiny, so why should I be concerned about what it means?

But I guess I need to rephrase "control over my destiny" because that's not very descriptive... because the word "destiny" is so misused. It's better to say I have no control over my own experience. For example, I remember on night, years ago, in Spain. I was traveling alone. It was nighttime. I had had a few beers. I had returned to my hotel with the intention of going to bed. But as I entered, I noticed a woman—not a young woman, but an "age appropriate" woman, as they say—sitting in the hotel lobby. I nodded hello to her. I could not tell if she acknowledged me. I got my room key from the clerk and went up to my room. I grabbed my laptop and returned to the lobby. The lobby had good WiFi and I often sat at one of their tables and worked on my laptop. Plus, I could order a beer from the clerk in the lobby. So just like the creek in front of Margaret Papadopoulis' house, I had a perfect excuse to position myself in the lobby near this woman in the hopes of striking up a conversation.

Of course, when I returned to the lobby she was gone. But I sat down anyway, ordered a beer and checked my email and such.

So, was any free will involved? Did I really "choose" to return to the lobby, or was I just acting out my fourth-grade male predator pattern for the infininth time?

I will tell you now, dear Reader, that I do not believe in free will. I do believe in awareness and responsibility, and in the inheriting of consequences, but ultimately, I was doomed to grab my laptop and return to the lobby that night simply because there was the image of an attractive woman sitting alone there that pierced my brain for about three or four seconds as I walked into the hotel lobby that night.

And if I am not accountable in such small decisions, how can I be accountable for large decisions? Maybe Thoreau didn't use the word reckoning because he knew we had no free will. Maybe he only asked for "a simple account" because he knew that we were only capable of being conscious. Maybe all he expected of us was to simply reflect on our lives, our patterns, our grand limitations, and our Icarus-like hopes to soar above our limitations.

Anyway, that's my pattern with women. I have pursued them all my life. I am mesmerized by their softness, their smell, their touch, their little quirks, their breasts, their pink or dark nipples, their hair, their pussies... If women were as sexually available to me as men are in the bathhouses, I would never go to the bathhouses. Well... I say that, but I can't guarantee that... but I would like to try that experiment.

Speaking of hair, let me just say, I love hairy women. Hair under the arms, soft sideburns, and especially hairy pussies. The more hair the better. I don't know why. I don't have an early childhood memory that I can access that explains that. But I do not like it when women shave their armpits or their crotches. It removes all their femininity. And a lot of the scent that makes up femininity as well.

Well, I see I have rambled on about women. But the fact is, all of that is in the past now... Like *Krapp's Last Tape*, the reckoning that one gives depends on the age at which one gives it. I am an old man now, so my reckoning about women is much different than it would have been at age thirty. (Again, this raises the question of what is the point of a reckoning at all, if it changes over time?) As mentioned, all of my sexual encounters with women for many years now have only been with prostitutes. So, what is the point of talking about patterns I had with women that no longer apply? I don't go to bars hoping to pick up women. I certainly have not met any women on Tinder or any other so-called social media. I don't meet anyone in my daily life who would date me. What other sexual choice is there for old single me except for prostitutes? Rich old men can delude themselves that the young starlets and socialites who hang around them are actually attracted to their gray hair and pot bellies. But whoredom is whoredom no matter what social level.

I prefer the brothel whores. It's a straightforward world, honest, clean, safe, and very satisfying. It's not love. In fact, it's a poor substitute for love. But love is no longer possible past a certain age.

The most recent prostitute I was with was a sweet lady named Lucia. She had come up from Venezuela to work in Jenny's brothel. Normally, Jenny would not hire girls from outside of Panama, but so many Venezuelan woman have fled the implosion of Venezuela's economy that Jenny took pity on some of them and hired a few. Lucia has two kids and, like so many other women in Catholic Central American, has little education and few options. I certainly can't save her; the most I can do is treat her nice and give her a nice tip.

I like Lucia because she likes to kiss. That's a rare thing in a prostitute, but she's new at the business. She'll learn not to do that in a few more months of working at Jenny's. But for the moment, she is still a novice. And I'm a sucker for kissing.

I could just lie in bed with her and exchange kisses. In some ways that's more intimate that fucking a prostitute that won't kiss you. But I fuck Lucia anyway, with a condom of course.

The only point I'm trying to make is that this is the best I can do at my current age and social situation.

It's just a fact—not a reckoning. I can't walk into a bar and pick a woman up. I can't walk into a room and turn heads. I can't walk into a nightclub and seduce someone on the dance floor. Those days, if they ever existed, do not exist anymore. These are just facts. And maybe that's all any reckoning is—just facts... the current facts of one's life, no matter how bleached and pale they appear when compared to the former facts of one's life.

CHAPTER SEVEN: THE LAST TIME I SAW EUROPE

I see that I have digressed again. I was talking about how the soft whisper of death in the scent of my urine this morning made me decide to go to Europe again. The only thing that nags at me about that decision—although it does not change the decision—is that I don't want to die in Europe. Because that would mean I would die in some hotel room, and there is nothing lonelier than dying in a hotel room, unless it's dying on the street in front of your hotel—just ask Chet Baker.

If I have to die, I want to die at home in Villa Rosario, in my own bed, even though it's not really my bed since the apartment that I have rented for these past fifteen years is a furnished apartment... but I have slept there so many nights, loved so many women and men there, that it feels like my own bed. And of course, like everyone in the world, I want to die "in my sleep", without knowing it, i.e., painlessly, unconsciously, and without the knowledge that I am dying. As an aside, that's what makes crucifixion so cruel—not only is it a painfully slow death, but you are aware the whole time that you are dying.

Yes, if I had my druthers, I would like to simply pass to the other side quietly in my sleep. But alas, the actuarial tables are against me. The statistics say I will die of a heart attack. How do I know this? Because I have a right bundle branch block—a congenital irregularity of the electrical wiring of my heart. It was diagnosed when I was young, so I've known about it all my adult life. It can be benign—two to four percent of people are born with it, and many people develop it as they age—but it is associated with heart problems (or "mortality" as the literature likes to say) as one gets older. To put it simply, the normal heart is wired so that electric signals that pump the heart go from point A to point B, like a train traveling directly from New York to Chicago, except that in my case, the train takes a detour through Washington DC first. The branch of nerves carrying those electric signals grew differently in my heart when I was in the womb. My heart still pumps, but I frequently have chest pain, and sometimes feel faint. And let me tell you, there is nothing like chest pain to make you think about mortality.

And so maybe that's why I'm so sensitive to signs from the gods, to the fluttering of angel wings, and to the scented whisper of death in my urine—because I've been aware of it all my life. I was diagnosed at age twenty, and I still remember the words the doctor said after he explained to me what it was. He said, "It's not a problem now, but someday someone may confront you about it." An odd thing to say, don't you think? I assumed at the time that he meant that some doctor someday might want me to deal with it. Now I think that he meant that I might have to confront my own mortality one day. Well, hell... there was no need to tell me that—I've been confronting it every day since then.

Whenever I feel that sharp chest pain, I wonder for a nano-second if this will be it. So far, the pain always passes within a few seconds. The wings flutter, brush against my face, and then move on. After all, if death is an angel, he or she must have wings and feathers, don't you think? So, death has been passing me by for more than half a century... but one day, I know, he (or she) will stop and do more than just softly brush my face with a feathered wing.

I would just prefer it not happen in a lonely hotel in Europe. Although that would be better than in the street, or on an airplane, or God forbid, in a restaurant. I mean, after all, I don't want to inconvenience anyone. Nothing ruins a good meal more than having someone at the table next to you fall out of their chair and turn blue, which is the color you first turn when oxygen can't get to your blood because your heart is not pumping. So, as lonely as it might be, I guess a hotel room is a better choice than any public place. I guess what I am saying is that I'd rather not die in Europe, away from Villa Rosario.

Regardless of the risk, however, my mind is made up. I will take one more trip to Europe. I haven't been to Europe in several years, and I miss the special kind of sensuality, energy, and debauchery that Europe has. As much as I love Villa Rosario and consider it my home, there is an energy in Europe that doesn't exist elsewhere.

I think.

I mean, that's how I experience it. But remember, I'm retarded. It could just be me—I could just be bringing this energy to Europe. But I don't think so. I remember meeting this cute transvestite named JoAnne in an Amsterdam gay bar. She was sitting at the bar in a man's shirt and woman's panties. I sat down next to her and we hit it off and started kissing right there at the bar. That does not happen anywhere else. At least, it doesn't happen to me. She and I spent some time together that night, and now, four years later, we still keep it touch via email. Maybe I'll go see her this trip. She lives in Germany, south of Stuttgart. She was in Amsterdam for the same reason I was—to experience that type of freedom.

Amsterdam is one of those cities where nothing encumbers... well, at least in certain quarters, on certain streets, in certain places. But it's a fucklot better than any US city. La Chorrera, about a thirty-minute bus ride up from Villa Rosario, comes in a distant second, because it has Jenny's brothel and a nice gay bathhouse. But as I say, it's a distant second.

I guess I want to visit Europe again because I have certain nice memories there... the transvestite JoAnne I just mentioned, almost all the prostitutes I met there, and all the bathhouses. There's an acceptance of these things in Europe. It's a live-and-let-live attitude when it comes to sex. But those are just my memories. I create this Europe in my mind, and so when I go there, I re-create it over and over. We create our world. There are probably Eskimos who dream of returning to Anchorage for the wild sex, and Oklahomans who dream of arranging another trip to Kansas City for the whores and bathhouses. I don't know. Certainly, the Australians flock to Bangkok. Maybe sex is a moveable feast. Maybe the mind is a moveable feast. In fact, I might be missing the boat budget-wise. It might be that my sexual dollar would go further in Bangkok, or the Philippines, or Buenos Aires... I just don't know. The Fates arranged it for me to experience sexual excess in Europe, so I think of Europe as my sexual Rumspringa. You see how it is? How we humans make our experience into a *fact*? It's like that old joke about how a conservative is a liberal who's been mugged, and a liberal is a conservative who's been arrested. Our personal experience—whatever it might be—becomes our carved-in-stone map of the world. I had good sex in Europe, ergo Europe is the sex capital of the world. It's insane, but it's how we map the world. And I actually mean "map". I know where the best brothels and best bathhouses are in Amsterdam, Madrid, Barcelona, Hamburg, Lisbon and many other European cities. I don't have to waste time—I've got decades of research.

Now... to be clear, just because I know these things doesn't mean I act on this knowledge. Just because I know where a brothel is doesn't mean I go there. You know where every restaurant in your town is, but you don't eat out every night, do you? There have been many times I have visited a city where I knew exactly where the best brothel was or the closest bathhouse, and I simply wasn't in the mood to go. The point is, there are places where nothing encumbers, and the fact that those places exist, that they are available to us *if we want them* is a very liberating feeling. You can linger at an outdoor café in Madrid for example, and have a second glass of wine, and ponder, "Shall I stroll down to such-and-such brothel, or shall I walk over to such-and-such bathhouse, or shall I simply enjoy this glass of wine and then stroll back to my hotel and go to bed?"

I certainly don't go to Jenny's brothel over in La Chorrera more than once a month for example, but it's comforting to know that it's there. Well, to be honest, I have gone there a bit more often recently, but only because Lucia is there, and I want to be with her before she becomes too jaded.

But the point I was trying to make is that there is a different energy in Europe, and that energy does make one think more about sex. It just does.

I remember the last time I was Madrid. Madrid has at least five bathhouses. There are three I particularly like, so I generally stay at a hotel equidistant from all three. But on this particular night that I am remembering, I was not interested in men. I was drawn more to women. Maybe it was because I had been strolling the Paseo, walking around, and the women all seemed like flowers in bloom, fragrant, colorful, vibrating and resonating with life... and it got to me. I have never understood what drives women to take such pains to look so beautiful. It can't just be the function of the capitalist-driven fashion business, because it spans all cultures. Are women like flowers? Genetically doomed to bloom as pretty as they can be while the drone bees work to gather the nectar to feed the queen to ultimately support the offspring of the hive? I don't get it. I own one pair of shoes and a pair of flip-flops. That's it. All women I know own more shoes than that. I wear one style of pants and only a few different shirts. I look the same every day. My clothes are clean, but the style is always the same. Women look wonderfully different every day. I remember a woman I knew back in the States who had two closets full... of just shoes.

Anyway, on this particular night in Madrid, I had been walking around, becoming intoxicated with all the different visions of women in the world. And that's how I ended up at this one brothel that particular evening. I had been there before so I knew where it was. It's a small place, just a doorway to the street, with just a small sign on the door indicating it's a "topless bar". But what a bar! The debauched details are not important—what is important is that on that particular night I wanted to be with a woman. Now let's consider this sentence... let's dissect this sentence.

"I wanted to be with a woman." I don't mean I wanted to simply fuck a woman that night. I mean I wanted to be with a woman. I would have been just as happy to have had a stimulating conversation with a woman at a coffee shop or wine bar. I wanted a woman's company, her attention, and I wanted to give her my attention. I wanted the interchange of energy. Sex was not the goal. In fact, in that particular bar, on that particular night, I said to the particular hooker that I had selected that I did not care if we had sex or not, but I wanted to feel loved, to feel cared for. It's the "girlfriend" experience that so many US hookers used to advertise on BackPage when BackPage existed.

And why, if I have had so much experience in bathhouses, do I end up longing for female attention? I don't have an answer for that. It might be the ebb and flow of sexuality—that great sea that gives and takes. Lord knows, there are times when I long for a man. I guess that just another reason why providing a reckoning makes so little sense to me—because I simply don't understand the forces that drive me.

But I did end up on that particular night, in that particular brothel, with that particular hooker going downstairs beneath the bar to a particular room where despite my claims of just wanting attention, we did fuck, with a condom of course, and I did cum, and I did go back to my hotel and slept deeply.

I do have to say, there is a difference in the sensation of wanting to be with a woman and wanting to be with a man—at least there's a difference for me. With a woman, it's the total package. I want to drink in her beauty, her smell, her way of talking, her physicality it's true, but more than just that, I want to drink her essence. But with a man, it's different. I don't want to talk. Either he has a nice dick, or he's dominant in a nice way (and has a nice dick), but bottom line, he has to have a nice dick. The exception would be transvestites or ladyboys, but then they have to be more like women with the attention. I'm not justifying all this; I'm just providing an accounting of it, a modest summation of facts. If some fat old hairy guy comes up to me in the steam room of a gay bathhouse and starts to touch my nipples and he has a big dick, well... he's got my attention. If he has a small dick hidden under those rolls of fat, I'm going to move away. That's just the way it is. But with women, it's different. The attention they show me makes up for any physical differences. Lucia, for example, is a heavy woman, and she's had kids, and her breasts sag a little. But I will choose her over any whore at Jenny's because she kisses me and she's attentive to me.

Of course, she's no replacement for Magali. Let's face it, Magali was the best. She had worked at Jenny's for about a year when I convinced her to leave Jenny's and move in with me. I loved her so much. I would have married her. But it just didn't work out. I'm not sure why. She had her demons and I know I had mine. We broke up, and she left Panama. I'm not sure where she went. She came back to Jenny's for a while, and she then left again. Jenny says she'll probably come back.

It's hard enough to love a woman. It's even harder to love a prostitute. Because we gringos assume sex is some kind of sacred part of love, and because we are property-oriented as gringos, we feel we have a right to own a woman's sexuality because we "love" them.

But I did love Magali. It just didn't work out.

Just like it didn't work out with my two wives back in the States.

Who knows why things don't work out between people. Maybe Carolina is right—that all relationships have expiration dates. It makes me sad to think that might be true, but certainly looking back, all mine have ended.

It's just that I see old couples holding hands or I

hear of marriages that last for sixty plus years. I don't know. Maybe they hate each other. Lord knows, I see so many bickering couples in my travels, it makes me appreciate traveling alone.

Anyway, the last time I was in Europe... well it was sexual debauchery.

But—as Mahatma Gandhi warned—what is the point of pleasure without consciousness?

Consciousness of what? That I'm going to die? That all of this is for naught? I would say that doesn't matter but then I see the gringos, even here in Villa Rosario, and certainly in Europe, pursuing pleasure blindly, without any manners much less consciousness, and I am offended and ashamed. I don't want to be like them, bragging about conquests, treating women like towels to wipe their cocks on, grabbing the tits at the clubs like they were toys... and it makes me angry. Even in the most aggressive bathhouse experience, no man ever treated me the way some men treat women.

If all gay men would turn hetero for one day and date women, I guarantee that women would never go back to their regular men again.

Well, I digress. The last time I saw Europe, I had sex in many bathhouses, and sex in many brothels, and I ate good food, and talked with good people, and rode modern fast trains, and stayed in nice hotels, and had a good time. So why wouldn't I go back again?

And, by the way, I submit that the way to judge a city, if not a civilization, is by the quality of the gay bathhouses they have. Ancient Rome was the best. All those ruins of the "Roman bathhouses" on those guided tours, where the guides simply state that the Romans just cleaned themselves and conducted business in the bathhouses... fuck that shit, those Roman bathhouses were gay, gay, gay. Gay in the sense that there was sex between men in those bathhouses. The Romans didn't have a word like "gay". Sex was simply something that happened. If you put men, naked, into a dark steamy room, they are going to have sex. They might be the most heterosexual men around, but they're going to have sex. All those circle jerks that happened in the Boy Scout camp-outs weren't because they were gay—it's because they were males gathered in one place. It's like that old Lenny Bruce bit (I hope you know who he is, dear Reader). He said that if being gay is like being a little bit pregnant—that if gay means *ever* having sex with another man—then he knew he was speaking to a room full of fags.

But I digress. I was saying that the way to judge the level of civilization in a city is by the quality of their bathhouses. Gay or straight, it doesn't matter. It's just a barometer. Amsterdam, for example. When I first started going to Amsterdam in the nineteen eighties, there were two gay bathhouses: Thermos I and Thermos II. There may have been others—I don't remember. But Thermos I and Thermos II had the monopoly. One was open for twelve hours a day, and then the other was open for the other twelve hours—a day and night shift, so to speak—the people used to call them Day Thermos and Night Thermos, but it meant that there was steam and darkness available twenty-four hours a day. One Thermos would close to clean up when the other one opened. Very efficient. Now there is only one bathhouse in Amsterdam, but what a bathhouse it is. I won't mention the name, but it has everything: a bar, food, Jacuzzi, steam room, Turkish heat room, video room, corridors of darkroom, private rooms, sitting room, everything. It's an extremely efficient bathhouse. And, likewise, Amsterdam has everything you need, and it's organized in a very efficient way. The Dutch are very efficient people. This street is for the skinny blond hookers; this street is for the older hookers; this street is for the ladyboys (and we will mark their rooms with blue lights instead of red lights, so you don't waste your time while you are browsing). Very efficient. And here is the bathhouse, centrally located, very well organized with condoms and lubes in these well-marked bins. You see, the bathhouse is representative of the culture.

Frankfurt has three bathhouses, with no-nonsense men who know what they want. There's an undercurrent of S&M in almost all German sexuality—I don't know why, but I feel it. And they have no embarrassment about it. One bathhouse even marks the different corridors with pictures of whips, and the number of whips tells you how intense the S&M will be. One whip is for men who like to give or receive light spankings; two whips means you like to be tied to an iron cross and whipped a bit harder... you get the picture.

Speaking of whips, Frankfurt has one bar that, although it's not a bathhouse, deserves mentioning. It's an S&M bar, where your entrance fee of ten euros gets you one beer and tied up, whipped, and fucked. Your choice of whether you want the beer before or after the fucking. Now that's emblematic of the German culture, don't you think?

Madrid has at least five bathhouses. None of them are as fancy as Amsterdam's, but as a group, there's everything that one needs—a place to relax, a place to bath, a place to steam, and a dark place to meet others who wish to be unencumbered by words or social contrivances. Lots of choices of size and layouts, many options, and likewise Madrid is a diverse city with something for everyone—just not all in one place.

Bilbao has two bathhouses, small, but adequate

for such a small city. Friendly clientele, a bit older, but friendly. And that's Bilbao. It's a simple city, older, nothing fancy, but friendly and very adequate. Sexuality is discrete in Bilbao. For example, the sex toy shops don't open during the day. They only open after dark.

Sevilla also has two bathhouses, but they are not well located, and not easy to find. And there is a certain schizy-quality to how they are laid out inside, as if the darkrooms were added as afterthought. Likewise, Sevilla is a city that is very difficult to get around. It feels like a very disjointed city culturally. I was never happy in Sevilla.

But the point is that the gay culture (as represented by bathhouses) is reflective of a city's strength and diversity and of its acceptance of the vitality that diversity brings.

Now, to be clear, I am not saying that the gay bathhouse is the epitome of culture or civilization. That would be stupid. That would be like saying that a certain artist was the epitome of a culture. I am saying it's emblematic of a certain tolerance and that that tolerance helps create a vibrant culture.

The fact is, bathhouses can be the loneliest places in the world, just like certain artists lived a very lonely life. Van Gogh is emblematic of the impressionistic painting time in which he lived—but he was the loneliest man alive. But nobody constricted his style of painting. In fact, when he went to the Saint-Paul asylum in Saint-Rémy-de-Provence, the doctor there encouraged him to paint, and Van Gogh produced some of his best works there. But the fact that someone or some place is great and talented and creative doesn't mean that there's not loneliness and pain.

Yes, I said it... bathhouses can be the loneliest places in the world. Sex without love is pretty lonely. It's better than being alone, but it's not as good as being loved. It's a paradox.

I guess I'm hung up on the culture of bathhouses because cruising as an act seems to me the perfect metaphor for how most of us journey through life. We don't know exactly what we want; we only have an idea of what we like. We wander around, hoping to run into someone who excites us, someone who can show us something new. We never come right out and say what we want—that would be too risky. We circle around the darkrooms of life, making eye contact, smiling, and occasionally, if it's dark enough, and if we're brave enough, reaching our hand out and touching someone.

There is one memory I must share that disturbs me a bit. As I've mentioned, there are many gay bathhouses that are open to women. Years ago, I was in one such bathhouse in Lisbon. There was not much happening on that particular evening—I had gone early and there were just a handful of men there and one middle-age British lady. She was there with a husband or boyfriend, but they weren't doing anything as a couple. When I met her, she was just sitting at the bar with a towel wrapped around her waist. Her male friend was in the steam room. I chatted with her for a bit and asked if she wanted to play. She said no, but then got up, walked down the corridor, and went into one of the gloryhole rooms and shut the door. In the wall of the corridor that comprised the wall of the gloryhole room there were, of course, several round holes. That's why it's called a gloryhole. I walked up to one of the holes and stuck my cock through it and she sucked it for a while. Evidently, she was one of those people who simply cannot admit that they want sex. She wanted to suck cock because that's what she was doing, but just minutes before she could not utter those words out loud. Of course, she was British, so maybe that accounts for some of that.

But I digress. My point was that I was at this mixed bathhouse in Lisbon on that particular evening, and there wasn't much happening. The only woman there only wanted to suck cock. So, eventually I decided to leave and go back to my hotel. I showered, got dressed, and proceeded to make my way out. Now, this particular bathhouse was underground. You paid your money at the street level, but then walked down a long flight of metal stairs to get to the lockers and the actual bathhouse. And as I was approaching the stairwell to climb up, I saw this old lady coming down the stairs. And when I say *old*, I mean old. She was bent over and making her way carefully down the stairs, moving in a very stiff fashion. In one hand she held one of those aluminum canes that has a handle and a part that wraps partly around your forearm above your wrist for extra support. In her other hand, she was grasping the stair railing very carefully. Her hair was all white. If you passed her on the street, you would have guessed her age as mid-to-late seventies. And here she was making her way into a sex club. There was no other conclusion. She would have had to pay the entrance fee to have gotten into the stairwell. She had a locker key grasped tightly in the same hand that was holding her cane. She had come to a sex club.

My first thought was admiration. "You go girl," I thought to myself. Maybe she liked to suck cock too. Maybe she would go into the gloryhole room, shut the door, pull a chair up to the round holes and suck any cock that appeared. I had no idea. Maybe she was demented or maybe she was a true independent. But I was full of admiration as I passed her on the stairs. It was only when I got to the top of the stairs and turned in my key that I realized I wanted to fuck her.

Does that disturb you? It disturbs me a bit. I didn't

want her to suck my cock through a gloryhole—I wanted to fuck a 78-year-old lady. I have no idea why—just for the experience, I guess... just to see what it would feel like. I wanted to pull back that flabby skin above the few white public hairs around that old pussy and see if I could fuck her. But I had already showered and thrown my towel and sandals into the dirty laundry bin, and I was already on my way out the door, so I didn't fuck her.

    But I wanted to.

And that doesn't jibe with my perception of myself as a sophisticated sexual person because, obviously, it's a bit perverse. I wanted to experience it just because it was perverse. Which brings me full circle back to the question of how am I any different from those middle aged (and older) gringos in all the bars in Panama City trying to fuck those nineteen year old hookers. Maybe I am perverse... I don't know. All I can do in this modest summation of things is lay my life out there and look at it. I have no idea what it all means.

CHAPTER EIGHT: WALDEN

One of the things I find wrong with *Walden* is the lack of sex. I mean, come on, he spent two fucking years out in that cabin. Did he never take anyone back there? "Why don't we go back to my place and I'll show you my bean collection." But no, there's not a word, not a whisper of sex, anywhere in *Walden*.

I like to think he was just being discrete, that he was living like a pauper out there on the pond's edge because he was spending all his money at the whorehouses in Concord. After all, Concord was only a mile and a half away. After a few weeks of selling his crops, he could have amassed enough coin to walk into town for a visit to Ye Old Brothel, don't you think?

"Oh, here comes old Hank again," the madam would say as she looks out the window. "He'll be wanting to 'ride the Merrimack' again girls, if you get my drift."

Maybe he didn't *choose* to live in the woods as much as he was forced to, due to his frequent expenditures at the brothels.

Maybe it was his editors who made him change his manuscript. Maybe he originally wrote his expenditures as:

    beans for seed.... $3.12
    potatoes for seed.... 1.33
    peas for seed.... .40
    payment to hos.... 540.00

and his editors made him change it to:

payment for a hoe.... .54.

    I like to think of Thoreau scurrying off to town under the cover of night, because it makes him more human, meaning of course, it makes him more like me. Not that I need his actions to condone my behavior, but at least it would acknowledge how we are driven by the same forces.

    Thoreau published *Walden* in 1854. The very next year Walt Whitman published the first edition of *Leaves of Grass*. At least Walt acknowledged sexuality. "Acknowledged" is an understatement—he celebrated it. Check out these excerpts from the poem *A Woman Waits for Me* from *Leaves of Grass*.

> *A woman waits for me, she contains all, nothing is lacking,*
> *Yet all were lacking if sex were lacking, or if the moisture of the right man were lacking.*
> *Sex contains all, bodies, souls,*
> *Meanings, proofs, purities, delicacies, results, promulgations,*
> *Songs, commands, health, pride, the maternal mystery, the seminal milk,*
> *All hopes, benefactions, bestowals, all the passions, loves, beauties, delights of the earth,*
> *All the governments, judges, gods, follow'd persons of the earth,*
> *These are contain'd in sex as parts of itself and justifications of itself.*
> *...*

Through you I drain the pent-up rivers of myself,
In you I wrap a thousand onward years,
On you I graft the grafts of the best-beloved of me and America,
The drops I distil upon you shall grow fierce and athletic girls, new artists, musicians, and singers,
The babes I beget upon you are to beget babes in their turn,
I shall demand perfect men and women out of my love-spending,
I shall expect them to interpenetrate with others, as I and you interpenetrate now,
I shall count on the fruits of the gushing showers of them, as I count on the fruits of the gushing showers I give now,
I shall look for loving crops from the birth, life, death, immortality, I plant so lovingly now.

1855 and Walt is writing about "interpenetrating" this woman with his gushing showers of semen. 1855... just saying.

(Actually... to be accurate, Whitman was always updating his book—almost every year—and I don't know which edition this poem was in, but the point is that *Leaves of Grass* was in the same timeframe as Thoreau.)

And I know that Thoreau was trying to convey something different, something totally different, but I wonder what he thought when he read *Leaves of Grass*. We'll never know.

Maybe that's my problem—that I was raised on both *Walden* and *Leaves of Grass*... so I have these two competing philosophies inside me: one that urges self-reliance, transcendentalism, simplicity, and contemplation of things; while the other lusts for "ignorant fuckery", as Allen Ginsberg called it. It certainly feels like a battleground inside me much of the time.

I'm worried though, that this recent awareness of death is going to put a damper on sex. This very afternoon, for example, I was looking at my calendar and pondering sex. Perhaps "pondering" is not the exact word. Let's just say I was letting my mind drift over my sexual options in the upcoming weeks. Obviously, for someone like me, sex is something that must be planned, because it always involves me having to "go somewhere" to have sex. And what are my options? There are always only three: Jenny's brothel in La Chorrera, the bathhouse in La Chorrera, or the Hotel de Sevilla. The Hotel de Sevilla is a beautiful gay hotel located near the beach down at Playa Lenora, but the trip there involves a grueling bus ride of several hours over mountainous unpaved roads. So, it's always out unless I'm taking someone there, and I have no one to take there. The brothels and bathhouses in Panama City don't even make the list. They are more expensive and further away than La Chorrera, plus there are more gringos hanging around there. So that leaves either Jenny's or the La Chorrera bathhouse. And as I was standing here in my little apartment just staring at my wall calendar and meditating on what I might do next week for sex, neither one of those options seemed to hold any appeal for me. I wasn't sure why. The British have an expression, to be "fagged out" meaning to feel tired, to be exhausted. Maybe I am just fagged out from having spent last night at the bathhouse. Maybe I need a day or two or three of rest. Maybe I need a trip to Europe.

Carolina often asks me why I don't use Tinder.

And I never have a good answer for her. We certainly have Tinder here in Panama. I think I don't use it because I can't. Somehow using Tinder would hit too close to home; would be admitting that I use women for sex; and that would crack my carefully constructed and totally artificial world where I believe that I'm different from all those gringo men in the bars in Panama City who barter with streetwalkers because I go to a brothel and pay full price without a quibble. Whenever I look at what type of men are on any of the dating apps down here, it's always fat old gringos with money looking to meet nineteen-year-old women. That's not to say that a lot of young women don't troll for old gringos, too. But I understand that... poverty and hunger are huge motivators. It's the men on the dating apps that I find offensive. And if I went on Tinder, I'd be one of them. And I don't want to be one of them. I might be one of them, but I don't want to think of myself that way.

But I have a good excuse. Most of the women on Tinder are not in Villa Rosario. Some are in La Chorrera, but most are in Panama City. And I don't drive—I only take the buses down here. So, to date someone in Panama City would involve lots of bus rides. I don't mind taking the bus to La Chorrera to visit Jenny's. Those bus drivers know me, and the ride is not that long. But Panama City is a different bus route. That's my "good excuse" for not dating. Silly, isn't it? But what can you expect from a retard like me?

CHAPTER NINE: OUTCASTS

In that same conversation that I had with Carolina (where she asked me how you can tell if someone is a good person) we got to talking about our mutual neurotic patterns in relationships. It's a conversation everyone has at some point in their lives, when they start seeing how they keep making the same mistakes over and over again... We all do it, you know—keep making the same mistakes. Carolina hopes she can change her patterns. We all hope we can change our patterns. But speaking strictly for me, I don't think I can change my patterns. That was the basis of my epiphany so many decades ago—that I cannot change my behavior, my way of perceiving the world, that I'm stuck with it, and that I might as well stop wasting all that energy trying to improve myself... that all I could do was watch myself, observe myself, and hope I didn't die stupidly. I know that sounds pessimistic, but I'm telling you that it freed me up, made me happier. I wasn't going to get any better, get any smarter, become any more handsomer, and certainly not get any younger, so I could just give up trying to dress up; I could stop trying to impress anyone, stop trying to be witty, stop trying to fit in... because I never had fit in, and I was never going to fit in. There was simply no place in this world where I belonged, and once I accepted that, I felt better.

The entire fashion marketing machine—in fact,

all marketing—is designed to present you with the illusion that if you just buy their product, you'll feel "at home", you'll fit in, you'll have a place. Buy this dress or this shirt, or get this haircut, or wear this perfume, or drive this car, or buy this condo in this neighborhood, and you will finally have a place where you can be you... and it's all bullshit. There are stores which just sell stylish underwear! Their premise is that if you feel their sexy underwear next to your butt, you'll somehow be your natural self and have more friends and be laughing all the time having a great time in your sexy underwear drinking wine in fancy bars with your fancy friends...

I have not bought new clothes in fifteen years. If I need clothes, I go to the equivalent of a Goodwill store in Panama City. Remember Thoreau? "Beware of all enterprises that require new clothes." It's true.

But, again, I digress. I was talking about how Carolina and I were talking about changing our neurotic patterns. She has found a new therapist and feels that she has a new understanding of herself because she is trying to learn from this recent breakup. She doesn't want to repeat the same mistakes. I told her that I was confident she could change her patterns; that she could learn to spot these loser men (and women) and not get into relationships with them; and that she could find a good man or woman and have a solid meaningful love relationship. I do think it's possible. She is young, intelligent, and motivated. There's nothing like pain to motivate you. So, I wasn't lying when I said I was confident she could change.

So why don't I feel I can change?

It's a paradox, isn't it?

I don't have an answer for that. Either we all accurately see the huge potential in others while remaining blind to that same potential in ourselves...

or we are totally deluded by other people's efforts to change and accurately see that we ourselves will never change. I don't know which it is. Shakespeare wrote: "There is a tide in the affairs of men, which taken at the flood, leads on to fortune. Omitted, all the voyage of their life is bound in shallows and in miseries." The usual interpretation of that quote is that a person has to choose to take that wave, like a surfer floating on the ocean has to choose which wave to ride... the old "free will" view. But notice the passive voice of the quote: the tide which taken at the flood... or omitted... Maybe the tide takes us. Maybe we're bobbing on the water, and here comes that wave of good fortune, and it sweeps us away... or not.

And here's another paradox: that in that same conversation with Carolina, I made the comment that relationships and love and being kind to people are the only things that matter in life. That at the end, when one is dying, if one is cognizant and able to look back, that the only thing that will make the view worthwhile is if one has been loved in one's life... nothing else will matter... everything else will be, as the song goes, an empire of dust... only love, finding someone to love who loves you, only that gives life any meaning. I told her that, and I believe that... but I do not practice what I preach. Is that simply because I'm too retarded? Or because the wave of love has not found me? Or I'm too inhibited to try? I don't know. It's just another paradox.

I, like Carolina, have had the good fortune to find good therapists in my life, and they have eased my pain... but it was a fluke that I found them... like most of my good fortune... just flukes... simple twists of fate, as the poet says.

Part of my good fortune was meeting Carolina. She is another outcast like me; a lover of both men and women, like me; a poet, like me; a world traveler, like me. So why aren't she and I a couple? It's probably due to the thirty-five year age difference between us. But it might also be because outcasts are always outcasts, doomed to always be searching for a place to fit in. Nonetheless, I hope she can find someone good to love who loves her equally.

The gods play no favorites, as Charles Bukowski was fond of pointing out. But they did allow me to meet Carolina and to form this bond and, thanks to Skype, we can talk and share no matter where we are in the world. And we are usually in opposite hemispheres or opposite continents.

I think outcasts have to be good to each other. We are the only ones who understand how it feels to be outcasts. Love does not come easy to outcasts, and so we value it more. One never appreciates what comes easy.

But I was speaking of change—about why I think other people can change (or in some cases, should change), but that I can't change. It's another paradox.

Suppose you live in humid Atlantic City and your arthritis is always bothering you because of the humidity. But then you move to Las Vegas where the air is dry, and your arthritis seems to disappear. Have you changed? No, you have changed your environment, and that change made you feel better. Maybe all personal change is like that. Maybe all we have power over is our environment. Maybe all we can do is put ourselves in a situation where we improve. Maybe that's what Plato meant when he had his ring engraved with: *It's easier to form new habits than to change old ones.*

Carolina broke up with that old boyfriend—or to be accurate, the break-up happened to both of them. That's how break-ups are, you know. They're like love—they just happen. One thing leads to another, and then another, and then suddenly you're in the middle of a break-up. You might tell yourself that you intended to break up, but in reality, it just happens.

Anyway, she broke up, but then she did a smart thing—she moved to a new town and got a new job. And her environment was suddenly different, with new people to date, better people to date, and suddenly life seems more hopeful. Did she change? Yes... in the sense she steered herself to a better environment.

Remember the parable of the mustard seed? Some people just land on parched ground and can't grow. Other people land where their environment is fertile, and they blossom. Maybe we're like the scattered mustard seeds, except we have feet and can pick ourselves up and transport ourselves to a better environment.

That's how I ended up in Villa Rosario. I left the States. I was suffocating there. My friend Miguel helped me find an apartment in La Chorrera when I first moved down here, and shortly after that I discovered Villa Rosario and moved here on my own. And I've been living here happily for fifteen years. And yet, and yet... I have to wonder if this environment is optimum for me or just comfortable. And I wonder that because I have to admit... I have not changed a bit since I left the States. I still skulk to the bathhouses under the cover of night; I still slip away to the brothels when I feel the urge; I still live alone; I still lament my situation but, in reality, do nothing about it.

Is this the best we can do? To merely change our environment so that we are more comfortable in our neurotic ways? Is that all I've done?

Even when faced with the prospect of death, what was my first thought? To go to Europe. And why? Because in that environment, I can ply my avocations more easily than anywhere I know.

I haven't changed at all. I am exactly the same as those fat old gringos in the bars in Panama City ogling the whores working the bar.

So why do a reckoning? If I really can't change, why am I wanting to change? Why do I find myself wanting to be better than I am?

CHAPTER TEN: REDUCTIONISM

If I had to reduce all of mankind's problems to one word, that word would be reductionism.

Sorry—a little joke there.

Well... I wish it was a joke, but it's not. The actual problem with most human communication (and certainly all social media and commercial communication) is reductionism. It has invaded and corrupted our thinking and our speech patterns.

Over the past fifty years, I have watched how both public and private discourse has been dumbed down to a one-sentence analysis to any problem. Sometimes it takes the form of two sentences: the first to reduce the problem to a single cause, and the second to prescribe the single solution. For example: "The problem with this country is illegal immigration. The solution is to build a wall." But usually it's just one sentence: "If you want to lose weight, just cut out carbs." Look up any subject on Google and you will see what I mean. All current language is geared toward a single-factor conclusion.

Not to be reductionistic myself, but I do blame the internet for some of this because most of the information we receive these days is via the internet. Remember Marshall McLuhan's *The Medium is the Message*? The vast majority of information we receive every second of every day is being downloaded to us in these predigested bits because that's all that will fit in the medium of the internet. The medium of the internet shapes the content. It's the "twitterization" of knowledge: Can this information be squeezed into 140 characters (or whatever the character limit is these days)? There is no space for any science or any lengthy dissection of an issue. The analysis has to fit on your laptop, and more often, on your cellphone. There's no room for science.

Take the average whiskey-drinking gringo, for example, and ask him, "Does drinking make you fat?" and he will laugh and point to his fat belly and say "Yeah, it does." But then ask him how. Well, he might say it's the calories.

But then you point out that a shot of whiskey only has seventy-two calories. Compare that to an avocado which has three hundred twenty-two calories.

And he will say, if he's a smart gringo, that an avocado's calories are mostly from fat, and that alcohol is a carbohydrate, and everyone knows that the body converts carbohydrates to body fat. The fat in avocado, he will add, is "good fat" and the body will not convert that to body fat.

You will ignore his comment and tell him that whiskey contains zero carbohydrates. In fact, no distilled spirit contains carbohydrates.

And the discussion will end there.

And why does the conversation end? Because the answer to why alcohol can (not will) make a person fat is complicated. Ask a scientist how the body digests alcohol:

> *"The liver converts ethanol into acetic acid, which can then be converted to Acetyl-CoA which can be used as aerobic energy in the Krebs cycle or used in the creation of glucose."*

Yeah, I don't understand it either. But it underscores the point that almost everything in this world is complicated. Which is why there are never simple solutions to a problem—because every problem is complicated. If it wasn't complicated, it wouldn't be a problem.

And if the topic of a gringo discussion has a political aspect, you can sit back and watch the reductionistic statements fly like bottle rockets.

> *"The county should allow supervised injection sites because it will save lives, prevent the spread of disease, and eliminate used needles in the parks where our children play."*
>
> *"The county should ban supervised injections sites and arrest all the junkies and put them in jail and force them into treatment. They are committing a crime. We are pampering them by giving them a place to shoot up."*
>
> *"Supervised injection sites have been proved to reduce crime."*
>
> *"Studies have shown that supervised injection sites will just attract more addicts to our neighborhood."*

It's one of the reasons I try to avoid gringos. It's bad enough that they can't open their mouths without expressing an opinion about something, but that opinion is always in the form of an over-simplified, single-factor analysis.

> *"The Panamanian government is totally*

corrupt. All the politicians are on the take."

"Ever since McDonald's opened in Panama City, the women have all gotten fat."

"Panamanians are lazy. It's just part of their culture."

"The problem with the new tax laws is that they favor the rich."

"All the women down here are gold diggers. They just want your money."

And once a gringo has uttered one of these inspired pronouncements, no intelligent discussion is possible, so all the other gringos at the table just nod their heads in agreement and order another round of drinks.

Whenever I overhear gringos talking, I like to fine-tune my bullshit radar by listening for the following phrases:

> The problem with X is...
> A recent study showed...
> It's easy to see that...
> It all comes down to...
> The bottom line is that...

Of course, no oversimplified generalization is complete without the speaker taking a condescending attitude toward the subject of his statement. That's a necessary ingredient in reductionism: taking a judgmental position over the thing you are reducing to a false syllogism.

And when too many single-factor statements get a bit boring, gringos like to dress them up with some expertise and some big sounding words. Sounding very confident also helps.

> "There was this study done at Oxford that analyzed the different diets of each country and compared them to the longevity rates of their citizens. It turns out that the people who eat low-fat diets have the lowest insulin resistance and live the longest."

Of course, I'm sure he never read the study. Some headline from some internet "expert" simply stuck in his head because it matched an opinion he already had.

It's true: Gringos love to take whatever reality they are discussing and reduce it down to one utterly stupid explanation they can gloat over. But what is the thing they are reducing? As we used to say in the sixties: what is reality anyway?

Thoreau said, "If you describe something as it really is, no one would recognize it."

Actually, he didn't quite say it that way, but that's my version of it. What Thoreau actually said was, "If a man should walk through this town and see only the reality, where, think you, would the "Mill-dam" go to? If he should give us an account of the realities he beheld there, we should not recognize the place in his description. Look at a meeting-house, or a court-house, or a jail, or a shop, or a dwelling-house, and say what that thing really is before a true gaze, and they would all go to pieces in your account of them."

But I like my version better. "If you describe something as it really is, no one would recognize it."

Maybe that's why I'm a writer—because you have

to use words to describe things as they really are. And to try and describe things as they really are is the most amazing feeling. Thoreau described it as like being in a fairy tale or the Arabian Nights. He was right about that.

I remember reading *God's Grandeur* by Gerald Manley Hopkins when I was in high school.

The world is charged with the grandeur of God.
It will flame out, like shining from shook foil;
It gathers to greatness, like the ooze of oil
Crushed. Why do men then now not reck his rod?
Generations have trod, have trod, have trod;
And all is seared with trade; bleared, smeared with toil;
And wears mans smudge and shares mans smell: the soil
Is bare now, nor can foot fell, being shod.

And for all this, nature is never spent;
There lives the dearest freshness deep down things: and
though the last lights off the black West went
Oh, morning, at the brown brink eastward, springs—
Because the Holy Ghost over the bent
World broods with warm breast and with ah! bright wings.

Hopkins wrote that in 1877, twenty-three years after Thoreau published *Walden*. Unfortunately, Thoreau died in 1862, so he never got a chance to read Hopkins's poem, but being the naturalist he was, I think he would have agreed with it.

I wonder if *God's Grandeur* is still being taught in school. I wonder if any poetry is still taught in school. I think poetry is one of the few ways to open the mind to reality, to how things really are.

But I see I have wandered far afield from my attempt to face my own reality—that reality being that I am old and the gods gave me a suggestion of death this morning. Ha! A "Suggestion of Death" was the name of the official form we had to file in court back in New York when one of the parties to a legal case died while the case was pending.

In fact, I have wandered so far afield that I've lost the thread of what I was going to say.

I think I have drifted from my intended subject because I am still pissed off about a conversation I overheard this afternoon. I had taken a break from this writing and had walked down to the open-air farmers market to buy some zapotes, and I overheard this one gringo telling another gringo about a recent trip he had made to Panama City.

> "Yeah, Mickie wanted to go over to the City and get some action, so he invited me to come along. He has that brand new SUV, you know. So, we drove over there to do some clubbing. He ended up parking by Plaza Santa Ana. It was a well-lit spot really close to the bars. Lots of people on the street, so we didn't think it would be a problem. And we had a great time at the clubs. Hooked up with some hot babes. But when we got back to Mickie's car, we realized it had been broken into. Mickie's expensive cooler was missing with all the booze. That was no biggie in the grand scheme of things, but then I realized that my Canon 40d with the thousand dollar lens was missing too. We called the cops, but of course they didn't do a thing. Didn't do nothing! All the cops down here are corrupt. Hell, they probably were the ones who broke in. I honestly don't care about the camera, but the flash card had eighteen months of

photos on it. I'm willing to pay a reward for my compact flash card. I posted a reward notice on Facebook and Craigslist this morning, but I haven't heard a thing."

I couldn't get away from those two idiots fast enough. There were so many things wrong with that whole conversation, starting with the fact that these two men are even here in Panama. First of all, I know the area around Plaza Santa Ana. It's not an area you want to leave your car in, no matter how well-lit or crowded it is. There are tons of bars and brothels in that area—that's why they went there. But there's also tons of lowlifes there just waiting for a brand-new SUV to pull over. Second, what the fuck was he doing leaving ANYTHING in a parked car, much less an expensive camera and a fancy lens? He's lucky they didn't take the whole car. And third, what did he expect the cops to do? The cops probably thought the same thing I did: if he's that stupid to leave something valuable in a parked car, he deserves to have it be stolen.

Anyway, as I walked back home with my zapotes, I was still upset about that gringo's attitude. He has no idea how wealthy he is compared to the people down here, and he has no idea how he flaunts that wealth in their face.

It's just another reason why I hate gringos. Every word out of their mouth is another nail to fasten another leaf of lies, falsehoods, deceits, and conceited opinion over the true nature of things.

So why have I gone on at length about reductionism and dumbing-down, and condescending attitudes, and narrow-minded gringos?

Well, part of my rant about reductionism was my just blowing off steam because of that gringo. But

I am also actually trying to get to a point, which is that the same "reduction-thinking" makes understanding relationships almost impossible. Not only are relationships incredibly complex, but people have lost the ability to discern complex systems. We can barely pick out the Big Dipper, while the ancients were able to map the cosmos and enumerate the Zodiac and even discern the subtle synchronicity of the stars and our souls. How can we, in our ignorance, navigate relationships? We've lost our compass and have to rely on advice columnists for direction.

What is a relationship? What happens between two people? Remember Don Juan's feeling of being picked up and thrown into the woman's arms the way a sailor throws a scrap of fish to a seagull? Remember the terabyte of information that was imparted through the fingers of the man in the Spanish bathhouse when he touched my chest? Remember Margaret Papadopoulis, my fourth-grade love? Something is going on far below our awareness.

"I loved her the first time I saw her."

Could it be that a part of us is talking to a part of the other person? Two unconscious selves talking to each other while the two adult bodies they inhabit are struggling to awkwardly say hello? Is that the "fate" that people feel when they meet someone that they think will be the love of their life?

The Transactional Analysis psychotherapists will say yes, that's exactly what's happening—that all of our childhood experiences, billions and billions of memories, each the size of a piece of dust, have been introjected by our childhood developing psyche and spun around inside us, like a microcosm big bang, and those dust particles have, with the gravity of years, collapsed and formed tiny planets, but the planets are alive, and they talk to each other and they fight with each other, and most importantly, they recognize the planets in other people... Well, actually, the TA psychotherapists will say it slightly differently, but the process is the same. We have these *characters* inside us, some good and some bad, and they connect with the characters inside other people, all without us having any awareness about it at all. What else explains the battling couple that stays together year after year, except that the witch inside her needs the warlock inside him to feel complete (and vice versa). The old adage about women marrying their fathers and men marrying their mothers has some truth. We have introjected parts of our parents, for good and bad, and we subconsciously seek out other people who have the corresponding parts.

Of course, the "corresponding part" takes many forms depending on how the characters formed. Sometimes we are attracted to people because we need to love them to complete our internal characters; but sometimes we are attracted to people because we need to kill them to satisfy the rage inside one of our characters. Like the couple that stays together and always fights.

So, I guess all of the foregoing was to arrive at this simple admission: that I don't understand my feelings toward Carolina. Whenever I start ranting about how stupid, crass, evil, and pointless gringos are, I always have to make a mental exception for Carolina and remind myself that if she can be so good, then it's possible that there might be other good people on earth. Another fucking paradox.

After she broke up with doofus, she told me that she felt so unlovable, and that she was worried she'd never find anyone good to love—someone good who would love her back. I was floored that she felt that way.

How could someone so smart, so pretty, so talented, so energetic, so intuitive, so alive, feel unlovable? She had only gotten involved with a loser man—a point I continued to make to her. Who among us hasn't gotten smitten by a loser lover? Sometimes it seems that the more fucked up someone is, the wilder they are in bed, and then the sex is so great you get sucked into their neurotic world. Doofus didn't have the right stuff, that's all. And she moved on. That was the right move. Yet there she was, feeling unlovable. It made no sense to me.

But then she pointed out that I act towards women as if I felt I were unlovable. I told her that was different. To feel unlovable is to feel unworthy of love—it's a self-perception issue. I don't feel that way. I think I am worthy of love. My issue is purely mathematical. I just don't think that there are any women out then who would accept all of my "peccadilloes". There used to be, when I was younger. But time has swept them all away. Magali was my last hurrah.

Yet, in my heart of hearts, I have to admit that I love Carolina.

Maybe it's the fact that we don't live together that makes it possible. I've always said that if I ruled the world, I would allow marriage, but would forbid cohabitation. Living with someone wears down the corners and edges that make people interesting. Familiarity breeds contempt. I think the high rate of divorce is entirely is due to people living together. How's that for reductionism?

CHAPTER ELEVEN: CAROLINA

I don't remember the first time that I realized I loved Carolina. I've known her for so many years that it feels like she's always been a part of my life, part of my daily routine. A mutual friend introduced us decades ago. Carolina had just returned to New York from extensive travels in Peru and Panama, and I was interested in picking her brain. I didn't see her for a year after that as she was off to India or somesuch place. But, somehow, we stayed in touch. I'd email her with a question or two and she'd always respond with a useful answer. She wasn't like other gringos who will give you an opinion when they have no experience with the subject matter. Carolina always spoke from experience. I liked that about her. Then somehow, slowly, as the years went by, we would text each other more often, and finally graduated to Skyping once or twice a week. Yet I still only actually see her in person maybe once a year. She's come down to Villa Rosario to visit me three times in the past ten years. I've gone to visit her all the other times—always in a different place because she's always moving.

When the thought sprang up in my brain this morning that I should go to Europe, the very next thought was that I should try and arrange to go there with Carolina... well, no, that's not quite true—my very next thought was that I hoped I didn't die in Europe. *Then* I thought about asking Carolina to come with me.

But traveling with someone is difficult. They say "he who travels furthest travels alone" but that's a metaphor. It's not really true in real life. In real life, couples travel further, because when you're with someone, you always have to *be doing something*, always going somewhere, trying out that famous restaurant, seeing that famous site, etc. That's why I prefer to travel alone. To me the perfect vacation is to go somewhere and just sit somewhere and absorb the vibe of the place. Skip the museums, the Eiffel Tower, and the famous castles. Just find a pleasant outdoor café and sit there—all day if possible—and just breathe in the essence of the day and the place. Of course, that's what old people do. We go and sit somewhere all day. People think we're senile (most of us are). But for me, I'm just gathering strength for any adventures that might occur at night.

But anyway, the point is that while going to Europe with Carolina was the third thing I thought of this morning—which means it was something I really wanted to do—it is a bad idea, and I probably won't do it. I think it would ruin our mutual regard for each other, and one should never do things that ruin mutual regard. It's true what they say about familiarity breeding contempt. Mutual positive regard, i.e., love from a distance, is a fragile thing, and it depends on that distance to breathe. It needs the oxygen that only space can give.

And I think our regard (Carolina's and mine) *is* mutual. As much as I can tell, anyway. When we Skype she always *says* she loves me, and I tell her I love her. Of course, as mentioned, we only actually see each other once a year, so it's an easy thing to say. I assume that real day-to-day love requires much more effort. Well, actually, I know it does. Remember, I was married twice. So, I speak from experience when I say that real day-today love requires real effort. It's not a passive thing, like pop songs suggest. You don't "fall into" real day-to-day love. You have to actively work on it. You have to make an effort to continue to love that person, day in and day out, year after year.

I couldn't do it.

I didn't have the moral discipline, or the moral courage, or the endurance, or the patience, or the wisdom, or the energy... I just couldn't do it. And so... I got divorced, using those time-honored excuses of time, external circumstance, and hardness of heart. But the failure was mine alone. I just couldn't maintain that constant commitment that proximity requires. I often say that I was worn down by marriage, but the fact is, I never had the edge to wear down. My moral fiber was already dulled and blunted. It always has been. It's just my nature.

So maybe it's the distance that lets me love Carolina so easily. Thoreau said that "individuals, like nations, must have suitable broad and natural boundaries, even a considerable neutral ground, between them." Maybe Carolina needs distance too— in order to love me.

At any rate, I can afford to love Carolina from a distance. And I can afford to dream about traveling to Europe with her. Because in my heart of hearts I know the truth: that I am not capable of real love. Oh, I can fake it for a while. I actually do a pretty good job of faking it—so good I often fool myself. Just like I can do a pretty good job of being a good travel companion for a few weeks. But eventually the mask slips, and I give into my innate selfish cranky deceitful licentious ways. There's no way I could be in Europe with Carolina and not slip off to the brothels or the bathhouses, and even though she has some idea of my proclivities, the sheer frequency of my sojourns would, I think, be offensive to her. So, it would be best if I went to Europe alone. That way, I could do what I want when I want. I wouldn't have to wait for anyone or be accountable to anyone.

Love creates obligation. That's why it exists—so that we will take care of each other. But that's also the main problem with it. Let's say you have a friend, and his car breaks down outside of town late one night, and he calls you for a ride home. What are you going to do? Tell him to fuck off? No. You drive out there and pick him up. He's your friend and you two have a mutual "favor bank" wherein you are both making deposits, because someday your car might break down and you might need a ride home.

But suppose some complete stranger calls you up at random. His car has broken down and he needs a ride to his house. Are you going to get out of bed and go pick him up? I wouldn't. I'd tell him to fuck off. I might be polite about it; I might lie; but I'm not going to make the effort to help him.

With a friend, it's different. You have a relationship.

Take that one step further: Suppose you're in a love relationship with someone. You don't even get to the scenario where their car is broken down outside of town. Why? Because why the hell would you let them be outside of town alone at that hour of the night in the first place? You're in a love relationship, so you probably drove them out there to start with so they could do whatever stupid errand they needed to do while you waited around to drive them back to town. After all, you're in a love relationship—you wouldn't want them to be alone out there at night.

I see that even with Carolina, even though we're five thousand miles apart. She tells me she's twisted her wrist at the gym and she's going to a Reiki healer to make it better, and I immediately start advising her to go to a regular doctor first and at least have it x-rayed. I immediately start trying to impose my world view on her... I immediately start acting like a gringo. I hate myself for it, but my reaction is immediate and without conscious thought. If her wrist hurts that bad, she should have it x-rayed. *Obviously.* That's what any rational person would do. That's what I would do. That's what any gringo would do.

But fortunately, because we're five thousand miles apart, she doesn't have to listen to me. She can do what she wants to do. She can go to a Reiki healer, or a fortune teller, or a soothsayer to fix her wrist. But imagine if I were living with her. There would be no escape from gringo logic. That's why I give credence to Carolina's view that most relationships have an expiration date. People wear each other down until they resemble smooth balls that slowly roll away from each other.

Of course... I say all that and at the same time I know that if Carolina asked to meet me in Europe, I would agree in a heartbeat. I would willingly be that scrap of fish thrown to the mouth of the seagull.

CHAPTER TWELVE: THE RESTAURANT GODS

Speaking of Europe... the restaurant gods have found me.

I first encountered the restaurant gods in Europe about eight years ago. I was walking up and down narrow streets, looking for a place to have lunch. You would think that finding lunch in any European city would be a snap. If it's anything that Europe has plenty of, it's restaurants... on every corner, in the middle of every block, often located right next to each other, one after the other, going on for blocks. Europeans love to eat. More than that, they love to feed tourists or to be more accurate, they love to make money off of feeding tourists. The waiters will stand outside each restaurant, each holding a menu, trying to catch your eye, sometimes even yelling at you like barkers in a sideshow. Any tourist who slows down to actually look at the menu will be cajoled in the language of their choice describing the succulent dishes that await them inside (or outside if they desire a table in the open air). It's a competitive business.

But I was speaking of the restaurant *gods*... they're a bit different. As I was saying, on the particular day that I met the restaurant gods, I was walking around some city—I forget which one—looking for a place to eat. I was hungry, and hunger always hampers my ability to think. Everything reverts to more primitive mental processes when one is hungry. And as I walked, I peered inside every restaurant, from the fancy ones with white tablecloths and sparkling-clean wine glasses to the hole-in-the-wall joints with three tables and plastic forks and knives. But none of them were right. Each one was too crowded, or too empty, or too dark, or too bright, or too loud, or I'd get a bad vibe, or *something*... and I would walk on. It was crazy because, as I said, the streets were lined with restaurants, and I was hungry, almost famished, but I couldn't find a single place to eat. "How could this be?" I wondered at the time. I wanted to eat, but no place felt right. It was then that I realized that the restaurant gods had found me; had encircled me; and were prohibiting me from making a restaurant selection. They were, in effect, paralyzing me.

Now, when I say gods, I do not mean good gods. Loki was a god, remember? Zeus had his temper and would fuck with anyone who crossed him. Even Satan was at one time an angel. And when I say "restaurant" gods, I do not mean that their paralyzing powers are limited to restaurants. That was just the name I happened to give them when I discovered them because, at the time, they were preventing me from eating at a restaurant. They *prefer* messing with you at restaurants because it's so easy. But they'll fuck with you anywhere they have the opportunity.

Now, before you think I'm a little crazy, remember that you've already accepted the fact that I can sense death in urine. So the idea that there are invisible forces that keep us from doing things isn't too far of a stretch, is it? And *you* certainly have a multitude of voices in your head, telling you that you're not good enough, or that you're fucked-up, or that you don't deserved this thing or that thing, don't you? Don't be telling me that you are not affected by your own self-recriminations...

Think of my restaurant gods in that same way.

Anyway, I was standing there, in some street, in some unknown European country, staring through the open door at some restaurant, feeling that this place was too empty or too weird or too whatever. And I suddenly realized that the feeling I was having was not coming from inside the restaurant, but was a feeling *around me*, like a dark cloud, a heavy dank fog holding me down... it was a feeling that *I didn't belong*... not that the restaurant was not good enough for lunch, but that I didn't belong inside that restaurant.

To be clear: it was not a feeling that I didn't deserve to eat; it was not a feeling that I was not worthy of that particular dining establishment; it was not a feeling that the restaurant or the people were too good for me; it had nothing to do with my worth as a human being. But it was a feeling that I *did not belong*, as if I was some alien from another planet who had created a rip in the time-space continuum by transporting myself to that particular street, and that if I entered the restaurant, the patrons would all look up at once and see that I was a space alien, and the rip in the time-space continuum would widen and expand and destroy the known universe. But that if I simply continued walking around, up and down the streets, no one would notice me, and the world would continue as normal.

When all this dawned on me, as I say, I was standing on the sidewalk, looking through the doorway into a small restaurant. I turned and looked around me. People were walking all around just like normal. I did not see the restaurant gods... but I could now *feel* them. I could sense their heavy presence.

But... I'm a rational man, not normally given to flights of fantasy. And so, at that moment, I decided to test my theory about these restaurant gods. So I stepped into the restaurant.

It was a small place, typical of many small restaurants in Europe, with three maybe four—tables, an owner, a cook in the back and a single waiter. It was dark, with a wooden floor and wooden tables and dark painted walls. There was one couple seated in the back-corner table. The owner was standing by the cash register about twenty feet in front of me. The waiter was setting dishes on one of the tables about ten feet from me. When I entered the restaurant, the owner and the waiter looked at me and instantly froze. The couple in the back were engrossed in a conversation, staring deeply into each other's eyes, and did not take notice of me. But the owner and waiter certainly did. The waiter was holding a plate that he had been about to set down on the table. The owner was looking up from some paper receipts on the counter in front of him. They both just stared at me without moving. I thought maybe they were closing, so I asked the waiter, "Abierto?" meaning, "Are you open?" He nodded his head yes, but continued to stare at me, as if he was seeing a ghost. Neither one of them moved. It was as if they were frozen in time. I stood there, holding my position as long as I dared to and then turned and walked back out the door. As I stepped into the street, I took one quick glance back at them. They were still both just standing there, not moving, watching me, caught in the time-space continuum rip, frozen for all eternity... at least, in my memory.

Well, that was all the proof I needed that the restaurant gods existed. If I had belonged there, they would have engaged in normal restaurant protocol. They would have smiled and greeted me; they would have gestured to one of the tables indicating where I could sit; they might have even ignored me and waited for me to select a table... But they did none of those things. They simply stared at me as if I was from outer space. I did not belong there, not there in their little world. The restaurant gods had made sure of that.

    I think one of the reasons that I like traveling, that I like moving around, is because it always takes the restaurant gods several days—sometimes weeks or even months—to find me. So, when I first arrive in a new city, I am free to eat at the restaurant of my choice. But eventually they find me, and the impediments begin.

    Of course, as I hinted, their meddling is not limited to restaurants. And the whole point of what I am trying to convey here is that last week they found me again—here, in Villa Rosario, they found me. We only have one restaurant in the whole town, El Balcón. Every other eating joint here is a soda, basically a food stand with some outdoor tables under a tin roof. None of Villa Rosario's eating establishments are worthy of the restaurant gods. No... they found me at the bus stop.
    I was just sitting there, waiting for the bus to La Chorrera. I had planned to head over to the bathhouse there for a little diversion when they found me and started fucking with my head. *Why do you want to go there?* they taunted. *Aren't you getting rather old for that business? What those pretty young men must think when you walk into the steam room, my my! You don't belong there...* you know, the usual crap that restaurant gods say when they are trying to undermine your intentions. Then they wrap their cold arms around you and drain all the thoughts out of your head so you can't reply. Finally, there is nothing left to do but stand up and walk home, and hope you can slip down to the bus stop on some other day and make your way over

to La Chorrera. Which—fortunately—I was able to do yesterday. The trick with the restaurant gods is to make your move quickly, before they can catch you. They cannot move fast. So, you have to walk quickly down the street and into the first restaurant you see, no matter what kind of food they serve. Make no eye contact and sit down immediately at the first open table. Once you are seated inside the restaurant, the restaurant gods are usually powerless to make you leave. Yesterday, I timed my arrival at the bus stop just as the bus to La Chorrera was pulling up. Once I was on the bus, I was home free.

But the point is that they have found me in Villa Rosario. They know I live here now. So now they can find me any time they want. All the more reason to take a trip to Europe. That would throw them off my scent for a number of months, maybe even a whole year.

And what does all this babble about restaurant gods have to do with my reckoning? Simply this: to show you how unworthy I am of this great thing called life. It's a constant struggle, you see. Last week I was unable to even do something as simple as catch a bus to the next city down the road, a bus ride I've taken a million times over the past fifteen years. I couldn't even catch a bus!

I know I've accomplished a lot in my seven-plus decades. I've traveled; I've written twenty-five books; I've loved; I've been loved... but when I compare my life to the lives of great men or great women... I am ashamed of how I have wasted my years. I couldn't even catch a bus. No wonder my soul yearns for places where nothing encumbers.

CHAPTER THIRTEEN: SOLITUDE

I suppose, in my reckoning, I have to acknowledge that I spend the vast majority of my time alone. Part of that is the occupational hazard of being a writer; but the greater part is simply my nature. But just because something is one's nature does not make it natural... or desirable.

Thoreau wrote: *I find it wholesome to be alone the greater part of the time. To be in company, even with the best, is soon wearisome and dissipating. I love to be alone. I never found the companion that was so companionable as solitude.*

I only share a part of his philosophy because I usually grow annoyed with other people after about fifteen minutes of interaction. Here's what he said about that: *Society is commonly too cheap. We meet at very short intervals, not having had time to acquire any new value for each other. We meet at meals three times a day and give each other a new taste of that old musty cheese that we are. We have had to agree on a certain set of rules, called etiquette and politeness, to make this frequent meeting tolerable and that we need not come to open war.*

So, I do agree with Thoreau on that point.

But unlike Thoreau, I do not love to be alone. I find it necessary. I find it productive. I find that it makes me think. It's the place where I can examine the meaning and value—or lack of value—of what has happened to me during my day. I find solitude valuable. It is the only time I am my authentic self.

But I do not love it.

I would not choose it except that it is the only place I have. To me, other people are far worse than musty cheese; they are nasty greedy self-entitled gnawing rats, always scheming how to take something from someone, or lie to someone, or cheat someone. Even the most banal of meetings is layered over with fraud and deceit, with each person trying to present themselves in the best light, to be well-regarded, or act as pleasant as possible to keep the transaction going, if only to lay a foundation for some future use and manipulation of the other. Women work on their appearance; men work on their voice, their expressions and mannerisms in a continual poker game of light conversation and story-telling, waiting for the cards to turn their way so they can take all of everyone else's chips.

Oh? Is that too harsh? Well, it probably is. After all, I've already admitted that Carolina is an exception... and if she can be so good, surely there must be others in this world who are good and loving people. I know there are at least a few—I have met them in my travels through this world. Maybe I'm just still fuming over those gringos at the farmers market earlier this afternoon.

But back to the topic of solitude... the reason I bring up the issue is that how we live usually determines how we die. Smokers die wheezing, trying to get oxygen; the hearts of gourmands literally choke to death on fat; alcoholics die of liver disease; extreme thrill-seekers usually die in some freak sporting accident; loving and generous people die at home surrounded by their loved ones... and solitary people die alone. There are many exceptions, of course. Anyone can step off the curb and be hit by a car. But the statistics are solid... and they are against you. In the mathematical world of probability, how you live your life determines how you will die. It's not rocket science. If you're a trucker, your odds of dying out on some lonesome highway are a thousand times greater than for some dude who works in a cubicle.

So, given this whole self-examination that my urine has foisted on me today, I suppose I should examine how I will die.

Obviously, I will die alone. (Remember that my one worry was whether I would die in Europe or here, but in any event, it will be alone.) I will not be surrounded by family or friends all singing hymns together to send me off to heaven. Even if I were to end up in a nursing home (unlikely since they don't exist in Villa Rosario), but let's say that through some fluke, I ended up in a nursing home or hospice back in the States, I would still be dying alone. Most people in nursing homes die alone—did you know that? Some six a.m. nurse discovers them when she comes on duty. The night crew saw the body at three a.m., but didn't feel like cleaning up, so they just wrote "resting comfortably" on the chart and left when their shift was over. Think I'm making that up? Ask anyone who works a nightshift at a nursing home.

Anyway, dying alone is a given. As mentioned, there is that heart issue, so statistically speaking, a heart attack is my most likely outcome... or maybe I should say *outgo* since I'll be leaving rather than coming.

Odd, isn't it? That when one thinks of one's own death, it is always a consideration of the "least bad options". It's never a choice between beautiful naked angels fucking you so hard you vaporize into heaven or getting a blowjob from a ladyboy that is so fantastic that when you cum God pulls you to heaven to recuperate... no, no, no. It's always a choice between anal cancer, pulmonary edema, or a stroke. Like a menu in hell: "Well sir, you have the choice tonight of asphyxiating in your own vomit or being crushed in a car and slowing bleeding to death while the firefighters fumble with the jaws of life." That's how we always think of our death: as the lesser of two evils. Or rather, as the least horrible of all the possible ways to die.

Shakespeare said it best: "As flies are to wanton boys, are we to the gods; they kill us for sport."

So why not beat them to the punch? Why not take one's own life with strong drugs and go out completely comatose? Make your own quietus with bare bodkin? Well... not me. First of all, there's a world of more fucking to do. As long as there is sex, I want to hang around. Not to be reductionist or anything, but sex makes life worth living. So, I guess that's one plus for the hedonistic, solipsistic, and satyric lifestyle: it keeps you alive. As long as there is the hope that I can get more pussy or more cock, I'll try and hang around. Ya gotta have a dream, you know.

But back to death... Leaving aside the absolute horrible ways to die that are possible here in Panama, like being eaten alive by a crocodile, or being stabbed with a knife in some botched street robbery and bleeding to death because there is no ambulance service... leaving those aside, and focusing only on the ways I don't want to die that are within the realm of probabilities... ...Alzheimer's tops the list, of course. It's statistically possible, as I mentioned, because of my mother, and it's horrible because you can feel your mental capacities slipping away. Although, to be accurate, Alzheimer's doesn't kill you. It weakens your immune system, makes you vulnerable to accidents, and increases the chances you'll die of other diseases or causes. But still, why quibble? It's a horrible way to go.

Thoreau's friend and mentor Ralph Waldo Emerson had Alzheimer's. At least that's my belief. The usual explanation in textbooks is that he suffered from aphasia, but I cannot find any reference to problems with his speech or language that is commonly seen with aphasia. But everyone, even he, noticed his failure of memory. He would say to Thoreau, "I feel perfectly well, but I have lost my mental faculties."

So... for the number one way in which I don't want to die, I would have to say it's a three-way tie between Alzheimer's, stroke or a brain aneurism. I don't want to be incapacitated, unable to make my way to the brothel or the bathhouse. I don't want to be shunned by the whores because of my drooling and slurred words. And I certainly don't want to be confined to a hospital bed, unable to move, unable to do anything but be aware that I had become a useless piece of flesh.

And I guess the number two way in which I don't want to die would be any other way.

I like being alive. And yet... death is coming. And, according to my urine, it's coming sooner than I want.

I need to plan my trip to Europe. Maybe I need to get my ass over there sooner than I think.

CHAPTER FOURTEEN: WHERE SHALL I GO?

I shall need some excuse to give when people ask me why I'm going to Europe. People always ask why. I suppose they are trying to be polite, or maybe nosy. Nonetheless, they will ask. Since I really can't tell them the truth (that I smelled death in my urine and decided I wanted one more thrill ride on the European sexual-go-round before I die), I shall have to make up a story. I shall tell them I have been researching the location of the lost treasure of the castle of San Servando in Toledo, Spain... an unfathomable treasure trove stolen from the Moors by the Knights of Templar and buried somewhere inside (or outside) the castle walls in the year 1215. I will tell them I have pieced together clues from various ancient texts and have created a map that I believe shows the location of this lost treasure. People who know me are familiar with my level of bullshit and will stop asking me any more questions at this point. That's the great thing about lying: most people can sense it and will intuitively take a step back and stop asking questions. And the people who don't have that intuition just give me an excuse to practice telling more and more fantastical stories.

But I do need to decide where to go. I suppose I need to go the US first. I checked the expiration date on my passport, and it needs to be renewed. I could do that at the Embassy in Panama City, but my New York

State driver's license also needs renewing. And I have to do that in New York. So I guess I'll go there first and get that done. Then I can fly from there to Europe. But where in Europe?

So many great brothels, so many great bathhouses... it's difficult to choose. I'm like a boy in a candy store, a phallus in wonderland.

Everyone should have something that inspires a childlike fascination in them. I think when you lose the ability to get excited with genuine anticipation, you become old and decrepit, like a dried-up broomstick of a person. And what is more anticipated, more exciting, than sex? And if I have to travel to Europe to get it, well... so be it.

But Thoreau's words humble me. He teased those who traveled far and never examined themselves when he said: *One hastens to southern Africa to chase the giraffe; but surely that is not the game he would be after. How long, pray, would a man hunt giraffes if he could? Snipes and woodcocks also may afford rare sport; but I trust it would be nobler game to shoot one's self. Direct your eye right inward, and you'll find a thousand regions in your mind yet undiscovered. Travel them and be expert in home-cosmography.*

But I do not flee to Europe to avoid myself. I know the limits of my abilities, the limits of my capacity for self-understanding. I long ago accepted that I was retarded, and incapable of ever achieving the ambitions that society had presented to me as if they were some holy grail. And certainly, the epiphany that I was retarded was the limit of my personal self-awareness. *A man's gotta know his limitations*, Clint Eastwood said, and I believe that. And my limitation is that I am incapable of tolerating, much less maintaining, long-term relationships. But too much loneliness is a bad thing. Even God recognized that. *It is not good that man should be alone.* So, I have made my peace somewhere in between aloneness and relationships, and that in-between place is sex... sex in brothels and bathhouses... i.e., sex in places where nothing encumbers. And so, I have come full circle to Johnny Kaufman's upstairs bedroom. Nothing has really changed. Even Thoreau would recognize that all we do in life is come full circle. *Our voyaging is only great-circle sailing,* he wrote. Although, given the funereal nature of this writing, maybe I should defer more to Eliot's lines: *In my beginning is my end.* Because I see that I have not changed much since those sixth-grade afternoons turning the pages of those Playboy magazines. I'm still longing for unattainable women while sucking very attainable cocks. Oh, well. That's life, I guess... or at least, that's *my* life... a tale told by an idiot, signifying nothing.

But... in the meantime, plans must be made, airline tickets must be purchased, passports must be renewed, and an itinerary must be chosen. So, the question remains: where shall I go?

CHAPTER FIFTEEN: A SMALL DETOUR TO TALK ABOUT GOD(S)

There is a myth as old as time that says that we humans are gods. The myth usually goes something like this: the gods are sitting around Mount Olympus feeling bored, so they decide to make up a game whereby they change themselves into humans and go down to Earth, but they remove from their human minds the fact that they are really gods. While they are in human form, they simply do not remember that they are gods. And the game is to see how long it takes them to figure out that they are gods... assuming they can figure it out at all before they die a human death and return to Olympus as gods. In some of the myths there is betting involved, where the other gods place wagers on how long it will take one of their kind to figure out the game. And this game goes on forever and ever, century after century.

A variation of this myth (the monotheistic version, if you will) is that we are the sole God... or some type of solitary universal consciousness... and that we are the only thing that exists—just pure consciousness—and every other person is simply a reflection of ourselves—some past version of ourselves, or some future possibility of ourselves that we have created... that we as God have created this illusion of a physical world with people simply to amuse ourselves; that this entire physical world that feels so real to us is simply a manifestation of some type of consciousness, like a hall of mirrors, where all we see are reflections of ourselves, that there really aren't any other separate people, just pieces of ourselves. Imagine that you are by yourself in a funhouse of mirrors, and that every mirror is broken, so that as you walk around you see a million other jagged fractured distorted versions of yourself—you can *see* thousands of people around you, but they are just reflections of yourself stumbling through this funhouse of mirrors we call life... That's the monotheistic version of the myth.

And this myth—that we are just a game being played by gods or God or some type of god-like consciousness—occurs in some form in every society, every culture, every religion, and every civilization. And my belief is that when a myth occurs that often, it's because it has some truth.

And it's a myth that has gotten under my skin lately. Why? Because every person I see or meet seems to have a piece of me. The Freudians would call that projection, of course... but what if it isn't? The Freudians were trying to explain why we always see parts of ourselves in other people, but what if they were too stupid to figure out that it was because those *are* parts of ourselves? What if those "intuitive moments" we have about someone else are just a realization about ourselves?

Personally, I think it's true... but the problem is that there is no one to shake us from our sleepwalk, no one to knock the scales from our eyes, no one to say, "*Well* done, *old chap. You figured it out!*" We just go on, stumbling through the funhouse, even with our dim suspicion that that it's all just one big sideshow and there's no one else here except our lone self.

But maybe that's the point of this reckoning... to shake myself awake, to remind myself that I am just a temporary visitor here, and that all these people I see are just versions of myself seen through a glass dimly. Maybe that's why I hated those gringos in the marketplace this afternoon, because they remind me of how debased my own attitude toward sexual partners is... and because I am ashamed of how I use women and men, I hate that same sexual exploitation when I see it in others. They say we hate the qualities in others that we hide in ourselves, and I think that's true. I am just like those gringos complaining in the marketplace today, and just like those fat gringos at the bars in Panama City ogling the hookers circling the bar. (But I do hate that they are so blatant about it; I at least try and keep it on the down-low.)

But what else can I do? I need sex, and I am incapable of maintaining a long-term relationship with another person where sex might occur regularly... so I have to resort to brothels and bathhouses. It's been said that the great Zen philosopher Alan Watts was *so close* to enlightenment, but that he liked to drink too much. I don't know what one has to do with the other, since there have been many drunken Zen masters... but the point I'm trying to make is that I always feel *so close* to some kind of enlightenment... so close, but my desires get in the way. I have not, as the Dhammapada urges, throttled my desires. Au contraire mon ami, as the French would say, I am full throttle ahead.

Again, another paradox: How can it be that both the throttling of desire and the giving in to desire completely—how is it they both get you so close to that same god-like state of ecstasy?

Once you start thinking of life as a huge game, it's hard to stop seeing it that way. For example, what if the movie *Groundhog Day* only got it half right? Instead of repeating the same day over and over again, what if our whole life is just one long day? Remember the Sphinx's riddle to Oedipus? What walks on four in the morning, on two at noon, and on three in the evening? Answer: a man. He crawls on all fours as a baby, walks on two legs as a young man, and then walks with a cane as an old man. What if all the years of our life were just one day to the gods? A daytrip for them, a chance to play the game, make some bets on the outcome, and try to work out the riddle?

Or, to approach it from another angle: psychologists have long pondered why it is that humans keep making the same mistakes over and over; why we keep repeating the same neurotic patterns; why we keep making the same bad choices... And they have many theories: early childhood trauma, Oedipal fixation, obsessive-compulsive disorder, repetition compulsion, unconscious forces, archetypes, repressed memories, self-actualization forces, addiction to trauma, you name it. But all of these "explanations" are really just descriptions of the behavior and the dynamics of repetition. They really don't *explain* anything! At least my theory that we are all gods playing a game explains why we repeat ourselves.

And what if part of the game is that every god is given a "distraction" to make the game more challenging? What if—to take the example at hand—what if I am a god who is playing the game, and what if my assignment (my avatar, if you will) was to come to earth in a highly sexualized body—totally preoccupied with sex—and to try and figure out that I was really a god and that sex was just energy? *What if sex is just energy?* What if my experiencing it as physical pleasure is just my particular distraction from gaining full consciousness?

Well... I fall short in winning the game. I just love sex so much! Probably too much. I guess that's what makes the game so difficult to win—or as the psychologists would lament, why change is so difficult: we are so addicted to our patterns, our vices, our distractions.

I wonder what the percentage is of gods who actually win the game. Five percent? One percent? All of us have met one or two people in our lives who seem to have figured it out—people who are so centered, so calm, so wise...but they are so few, so very few.

And I wonder if part of the game is that the gods—the ones up on Olympus betting on (or against) us players down below—I wonder if they are allowed to send hints down to the players. Maybe these little events that happen to us, these events that give us pause and make us think; these "cubic centimeters of chance" as don Juan Matus called them... I wonder if they are clues that the gods send down to help us figure out the game. And likewise, maybe the gods who are betting against us are allowed to send down obstacles to thwart our enlightenment, maybe in equal proportion to the clues that the gods betting in our favor send. Say, for example, one god sends you the absolute love of your life, the one person who proves that love is the best thing in the world—are the gods betting against you allowed to kill that person in a freak traffic accident, just to give you an obstacle in the game? Does that sound far-fetched? No different from the Church which for centuries has taught that "God works in mysterious ways." Is my explanation any more ludicrous than any religion?

Maybe my intimation of death is one of those clues. Maybe the smell of death in my urine this morning was a message from the gods reminding me that time is short, that the game is almost over, and that there's a lot of money riding on what I might do next. Will I go to Europe, to the places where nothing encumbers, and try once again to immerse myself in flesh and fluids, to overwhelm my senses, to drown in cock and breasts and pussy, to experience that physical ecstasy of sex that comes so close to the sensation of godliness... or will I wake up and realize a whole different level of godliness instead—some type of consciousness that I can't even conceive of right now?

Intellectual enlightenment? Is that even possible? Is it possible to figure out the game through intellect alone? I somehow doubt it... and yet, isn't that exactly what I've been trying to do here? What is the point of a written reckoning if not to intellectually goad and confront the mind to realize what a huge fucking sideshow this has all been?

And yet... where does this all get me? I have not changed in the six decades since Johnny Kaufman's bedroom. I'm not going to change now. I love sex. I need sex. I think about it all the time. I want it in Villa Rosario; I want it in La Chorrera; I want it in Europe. It's gotten harder to get the older I've become, but my desire for it has not diminished. Maybe my sexual cravings are part of my godliness. Maybe the gods *are* the sex-crazed creatures that mythology says they are. Am I Zeus, changing myself into a swan to fuck the mortal woman Leda? I certainly seem to play the chameleon in order to get sex. Am I a sex-crazed god simply inhabiting a man's body, or am I a god assigned to play a sex-obsessed man? I don't know.

But it brings me full circle to the question of what separates me from the herd of old thick white-haired gringos ogling whores in the bars or cruising in rented SUVs for rentboys in the zócalo after dark. If I am a god, then either those gringos are gods or they are all just fragments of me in this house of mirrors.

I *feel* different than those other gringos... but I don't know. I wish I understood it all... but I am retarded... which is to say... I am human. I may have been a god once... I may be a god now... but I just feel like a retard.

All I know for sure is that death is coming. My urine told me that. And then I decided to go to Europe. Those are the facts. And so, being stuck in my repetitive wheel, I shall go to Europe. Maybe Sartre was right: I'm just like Pierre in *Les Jeux Sont Faits*, unable to stop my repetitive ways despite having godlike knowledge.

CHAPTER SIXTEEN: FISH OR CUT BAIT

Villa Rosario, like all cities down here, was built around a large Catholic church. I can see the bell tower from my balcony, and more importantly, I can hear the bells. They count out the hours on each hour and ring once on the half-hour. They ring for morning mass and evening mass. They ring incessantly at Christmas and Easter.

But there's a special bell for funerals. A solitary, low-sounding mournful bell, muted and somber, that rings with long pauses between peals.

It's been ringing this afternoon. Someone has died, and people are gathering in the Church for a service. Afterward, they will carry the body to the cemetery for burial.

Just another reminder from the universe. Another reflection in the funhouse hall of mirrors, signaling death.

Time to get busy living. Time to fish or cut bait. Time to decide where to go in Europe.

As mentioned, I need to go to the States first. My passport and my New York driver's license need renewing, and I need to meet with my tax accountant and my publisher. So I'll go to New York first. Besides, I can visit the few friends still alive back there. Then, when I finish my business, I can fly to Europe from New York with my new passport.

But from New York to where? Amsterdam is

always the path of least resistance from New York. It's one the cheapest flights, and the Schiphol Airport is so well-organized. Down the stairs from Immigration is the train that whisks you to Amsterdam Central, and a two-minute walk to my favorite hotel in the red-light district. Then, after a week or two in Amsterdam, it's easy to work my way south to Spain and Portugal.

But for some reason I've been thinking about Barcelona recently. I could fly there first, and then perhaps wander up to Amsterdam.

I suppose the logical thing to do is to look at the whole trip, from New York to Europe and then from Europe back home to Panama. There's no predicting airplane ticket prices anymore. It might turn out to be cheaper to fly from New York to Barcelona and then fly back to Panama City from Amsterdam, even though it's the longer route. Who knows?

That would be the obsessive-compulsive's logical thing to do—to look at the most economically feasible route. But the other way to plan would be to pick the place that my heart wants to see first and go there, regardless of whether that made for a more expensive route.

It's easy to be logical; it's acceptable to be a little OCD; it's prudent to be fiscally responsible; but it's difficult to know what your heart wants.

This trip to Europe feels like a big deal, so in keeping with Freud's suggestion of trusting one's heart with large matters, maybe I won't look at the cost. Maybe I'll just focus on where I want to go first. After all... if my urine is right, this might be my last trip to Europe.

The last trip... I am reminded of D.H. Lawrence's words in his *Ship of Death:*

> *And it is time to go, to bid farewell*
> *to one's own self, and find an exit*
> *from the fallen self.*

And if this is my last trip to Europe, then really... what the fuck does it matter what it costs? I could put it all on a credit card and fly ultra-first class and die without ever having to pay a dime.

But maybe the gods don't want to kill me yet... maybe they just want to prod me with the idea of death so that I would undertake this self-examination. Maybe they want me to change.

What an odd thought... We always think that personal change is something we have to undergo ourselves; something we need to decide for ourselves after long and arduous self-examination... but what if it's not? What if it's something the gods want us to do so that we will be happier, so that we will be more god-like?

How would I be different? Would I be more kind, more understanding? I have no idea.

Sometimes I play a mental game where I try to imagine what I might do instead of being a writer, if I had my whole life to do all over again. Sometimes I see myself as a lone gold prospector, living solitary in a camper van up in the mountains, prospecting for gold in ancient creek beds. Sometimes I see myself as a young architect, designing fantastic new buildings. Sometimes I imagine I have magical powers... but mostly I see myself just as I am, as a writer, perhaps a bit more successful, but as a writer nonetheless. It's a lot like prospecting for gold in ancient creek beds, living alone in my small apartment. I certainly find more nuggets than any actual gold prospector. And what I do is a lot like designing fantastic structures that soar up to the heavens. I certainly have written more twists and secret passages than Gaudi ever built. And it's very much like having magical powers. Being a writer is the most amazing occupation ever. I mine gold, design amazing story edifices, and have the most amazing superpowers. No... if I had my life to live all over again, I would do exactly what I do now. Write.

But I do wish I had been kinder to people. It would have been kinder, for example, to have been honest with both my wives about the kind of man I am. It would have been kinder not to have married them. But then I would have missed out on all that they added to my life... It's another paradox, isn't it? If I, like George Bailey in *It's a Wonderful Life*, had not existed in the lives of my two ex-wives, I would not have done the hurtful things to them that I did—that's true—but I would not have brought them what love I did bring them, and they would not have brought me the love they brought me. They would have suffered, with or without me. It's the nature of life to suffer. As Buddha said, we *will* lose all that we love. Not loving doesn't reduce suffering. Not loving only increases suffering.

I should have loved *more*.

It occurs to me that if there really all gods up on Olympus, if we are indeed gods in human form, if I am a god, if the gods are sending me clues, if the scent of death in my urine is a sign that death is near, if death is an advisor, if there is money riding on what I might do next... if any or all of these things are true, then maybe what all this means has less to do with dying soon and more to do with acting more godlike with the time I have left. Maybe the clue that the gods are sending is that I should stop mucking about and start acting like the god I really am. I mean, why send me clues if there was no time left to start acting better? I'm not talking amount of time, but rather the quality of time. Clearly there's not much time left—I'm old. But maybe I should start acting kinder, loving more, being more heartfelt in my contact with people... I simply don't know what else to make of it all. That's the only thing my poor retarded self can come up with. I don't want to be a worse person than I am now; I don't want to be the same person I am now; so the only choice left is to be a better person than I am now.

In *Memory Gardens*, Allen Ginsberg wrote:

> *Well, while I'm here,*
>   *I'll do the work—*
> *and what's the Work?*
>   *To ease the pain of living.*
> *Everything else, drunken*
>   *dumbshow.*

Maybe that's all we can do in life, to ease the pain of living, to try and love other people a bit more, and to try and let them love us.

"Maybe that's all we can do in life." Maybe we have no control over any of the events in our lives—only control over how we treat others. I've never been able to alter my sexual preferences—my slithering down late-night streets, quietly looking for the unmarked door that leads to steamy dark rooms full of naked men; or my frequenting brothels where women sit bored in bikinis on long sofas staring at cell phones waiting until the next client enters. Maybe my patterns and preferences were set in sixth grade in Johnny Kaufman's bedroom, staring at pictures of naked unattainable women while sucking cock; or maybe they were set long before I stepped into his bedroom, set deep down in my DNA, back through generations. I don't know. I only know that my desires and patterns are set in the strongest concrete possible—the human mind.

To paraphrase the opening lines of the Dhammapada: Mind precedes all mental states. Action follows Thought the way the cart wheels follow the ox. And Suffering follows Action the way the cart wheels cut ruts into the dirt road.

I can't change my desires. I can't even change the thoughts that pop into my head. I can't change the thrill that sex brings. I am just like those gringos in the bars in Panama City, except I am more discrete, more secretive. The only thing I can change is how kind I am to people. I think that's all the power I have over my fate. My only free will is whether I am kind to others. Everything else in my life is out of my control. Only making the conscious effort to care—to be kind—is within my control.

Maybe that's how human life is designed. Maybe that's the game the gods play. All our free will is an illusion except our ability to be kind.

I will go to Europe. I have no choice. I smelled death, and my mind immediately formed the Thought of Europe. So, I will go to Europe. My actions will follow my thought like the cart wheels following the ox. I have no choice. And once I get there, I know myself—I will visit the bathhouses and brothels that I love, and maybe finds some new ones to explore. I will repeat my actions over and over, as I have always done, and as I will always do, until I die. Only maybe this time, I will try and be kinder to everyone I meet.

The Dalai Lama once said that he had only one religion, and that was *kindness*. That makes sense to me; that feels right. Everyone we meet carries such a heavy burden. All of us labor under the forgetful delusion that we are not gods; all of us think this life is real and important; all of us have forgotten ourselves. Only a moment of kindness seems to awaken a dim light of consciousness for a moment—a consciousness of some vast ocean of something else around us, something we used to know but have forgotten.

CHAPTER SEVENTEEN: FREE WILL

Samuel Johnson, the great English writer of the 1700s, is reputed to have emerged disgruntled from a lecture on metaphysics—a lecture where the speaker propounded that the universe didn't exist, that it was all a creation of our consciousness. And his buddy Boswell, who had been with him at the lecture, asked Sammy how he refuted the lecturer's argument. Supposedly, Sammy stamped his foot loudly on the ground and shouted, "I refute it thusly!"

It's a cute story, but I am not convinced. I know that the ground feels hard, but my own experience with life is much more ephemeral. I experience life as a dream most of the time. Maybe that's simply my limited capacity as a retard, simply a function of not enough folds in my cerebral cortex. Yet, consider the words of the great Chinese Taoist teacher Chuang Chou (aka Zhuang Zhou), from the fourth century BC:

> Once upon a time, I dreamed I was a butterfly, fluttering hither and thither, for all intents and purposes a butterfly. I was conscious only of my happiness as a butterfly, unaware that I was Chuang Chou. Soon I awoke, and there I was, veritably myself again. Now I do not know whether I was then a man dreaming I was a butterfly, or whether I am now a butterfly, dreaming I am a man.

So, maybe I'm not the only retard around.

Because what I'm talking about here is the *physical* experience of life, from one moment to the next. It all simply *feels* like a dream to me. Each scene shifts into another scene like liquid. People walk up to me and then disappear. I awake, move around, sleep, then wake again. Clearly, I'm not the only one who feels this way. *All the world's a stage,* Shakespeare wrote, *and all the men and women merely players.*

But, like Samuel Johnson, I suppose I have to deal with the hard ground (even if it is a dream). And so, a few minutes ago, I got online and reserved a plane ticket to New York—one way. My passport expires in eight months, and many countries won't let you in if there is less than six months' time left on your passport. So I might as well go ahead and renew it for another ten years, along with my New York driver's license... so off to New York I will go. Ha! How's that for hedging my bets? How's that for talking out of both sides of my mouth? Here I am, intuiting death in my urine, and then ergo deciding that I *must* go to Europe for one more fling before Death taps me on the shoulder, and in the same breath saying I have to go to New York first to renew my passport for *another ten years*! How's that for blind optimism? For good old gringo American spirit? For denying mortality?

Well... yes. I am hedging my bets... because I don't want to die. And I hope that I am mistaken about the hint of death this morning. I am, after all, a practical man. And so I will render unto Caesar the fees necessary to renew my passport and get my papers in order, so that hopefully I can visit Europe many times; and I shall render unto God the things that are God's and make love to as many people—men and women—

as I find attractive. And I will do so with an enthusiasm befitting one's last time at debauchery. Yes, I will hedge my bets; I will talk out of both sides of my mouth; and I will cover my ass. I don't make the rules—I just try and slide by them.

So, I have begun. I have my ticket for the first leg of my trip (no pun intended; I certainly hope it's not a fall). As soon as I get my new passport, I will book a flight to Europe from New York. My time is my own, so I can spend a month or two in Europe if I wish, and then I will fly back home to Panama.

And in the meantime, I can enjoy the process of deciding which route to take. For it is true of travel more than any other activity: that the planning and anticipation are as good—and sometimes better—than the actual journey. I am starting to long for Amsterdam already, with its ladyboys down on Barndesteeg Street; the wonderful huge bathhouse with its refined clientele; the bars with the basement darkrooms with the less refined clientele; the Thai massage parlors with the printed sex menus listing activities and prices (all with complimentary tea); and sprawling Madrid, with its choice of bathhouses each with different types of men; the hard-edged hookers up and down the Calle de la Montera, too dangerous to actually pick up, but so wonderful to watch as they ply their trade to the tourists while I sit at a nearby outdoor café enjoying a glass of wine observing the parade; and graceful Barcelona with its discrete brothels; Frankfurt with its S&M brothels; and Lisbon with its coed sex clubs. Europe is such a cornucopia, a cockucopia, and a cuntucopia... I can hardly wait.

Maybe sex is to me what the solid ground was to Samuel Johnson—a way of refuting any intellectual argument on the meaningless of life. Ha!

Another paradox... using meaningless sex to refute the meaninglessness of life.

But maybe that's where the aforementioned kindness comes in, as the only *true* antidote to the meaninglessness of it all. Maybe the phenomenon we name as "kindness" is actually something else. Maybe it's not just a feeling, not just sentimentality, but an actual type of consciousness. For what does it mean to "be kind" to someone else? Does it not mean that first I must experience their world, put myself in their shoes... not so much to "understand their point of view" (because most people's point of view is small, stupid, and selfish) but to understand how they could not help but come to their narrow point of view? Because they—like me—have had no free will in their life. They inherited their genetics, their circumstances, their fate. They too are gods who were hurled down to earth without memory or consciousness of their god-like state; They too were each assigned a task, a lesson in life if you will, a challenge to cope with, so that the other gods could place bets on whether they would wake up to their true identity.

There is no free will, my friend, not in the sense we use the term. What I "choose" to have for breakfast is totally dependent on my options—what's in my refrigerator—plus layers upon layers of memory and experience that make up the psychological state of being we call "what would I like for breakfast?" The very thoughts and images that pop into my head are created by my Mind, and I respond to them as automatically as Pavlov's dogs to the bell. I think when Thoreau asked, *If the bell rings, why should we run?* he was speaking rhetorically. Because the answer is, *because we are programmed to do so.* We have no choice. Just like me pretending to hunt for crayfish in the creek by Margaret Papadopoulis's house or taking my laptop down to the lobby at that hotel in Spain on the hope of positioning myself near that woman I briefly saw sitting there. I had no choice in those decisions. The desire sprung into my mind. I embraced the desire. How could I not? It is my nature. My mind assessed the options and chose the one with most plausible deniability and I followed blindly. That is the pattern of my life. No different than the intimation of death popping into my mind this morning, and my mind assessing the situation and immediately choosing to go to Europe—the option with the most sex and the most plausible deniability. I will tell my friends that "it's just a vacation", just a break from the rainy season that will soon descend upon us here in Panama. And to any acquaintances I can just say that I'll be traveling to do research for another book. And to any gullible gringo I will spin some bullshit about researching the lost treasure of San Servando in Spain. Plausible deniability is important. It would not do to simply tell anyone the truth.

My mind is good—it's not going to pick an option that puts me in danger. It's going to pick a feasible objective, one that I can afford and can manage. But just because a plan is feasible, doable, fun, affordable, satisfying, enjoyable, etc., does not mean it has anything to do with free will. A dog that wants discourse of reason would enjoy his breakfast just as much.

But kindness... that's different. I don't know how or why, but it is. Maybe *that's* the cubic centimeter of chance that don Juan Matus was trying to tell Carlos Castaneda about. Maybe that's the crack in the matrix—the ability to have a moment of kindness with someone else. For example, suppose you're at the grocery store making idle conversation with the cashier who is ringing up your items. You know it's idle conversation by the content ("Did you find everything you were looking for today?") and by the fact that there is no eye contact. But suppose you break the pattern and say, "Well, I was hoping to find a hundred dollar bill on the floor, but I didn't", she will look up, startled at the unorthodox response. Then you have eye contact; then you have a chance to smile and say something kind. I'm not talking about flirting—I'm just talking about acknowledging her presence, her existence in the world... just a word, a question, a compliment, nothing more, but something that breaks the collective sleepwalk that we all are in—something, as don Juan Matus said, that *stops the world*, if only for a moment. Maybe that's all kindness is—just a brief awakening from the sleepwalk of life.

I just don't experience myself as having any more power than that in my life. All of my decisions, even the life-changing ones, were just an automatic response to the options that life offered: my decision to get divorced (twice), my decision to go to rehab, my decision to drink again, my decision to be a writer, my decision to move to Panama. There was no choosing those paths, because there is no free will. Each of those decisions was made for me by my Mind as the best option open to me at the time.

But kindness... I think that's another matter. I think the gods must have constructed the universe to leave kindness as a hidden power in the niches of life, the same way that code writers put hidden powers in video games.

Maybe I'm crazy... after all, I believe in messages from urine and betting gods... but that's how life feels to me; that's my direct experience of life—that the moment-by-moment ability to stop what we are doing and just look at someone else and actually see them and to say something kind, to acknowledge their godliness in the world... that feels like the only power we have, the only free will.

CHAPTER EIGHTEEN: POINTLESSNESS

It is evening now, and I come to the end of my reckoning. And what have I discovered? To be honest, absolutely nothing. There's nothing I've uncovered that I didn't already know about myself. Isn't that the way it always is? Isn't that the way it is for you?

Ever grab one of those "self-help" books from the shelf at a bookstore or library and open up a random page and just read it? I always find myself nodding my head and thinking, "Yes, that's true," in the sense that I recognize something that I already know is true. Life is short? True. Try and do what makes you happy? True. Being in love is the best thing in the world? True. Life is hard? True... the list goes on and on. And if I were a list, I would simply say I love sex; I've always loved sex; I don't handle commitment well; I've have not always been honest with people; I would like to be more kind. True, true, true... So where does all this get me? I have spent this entire day scribbling madly, trying to make sense out of an overwhelming intuition that death is coming. But I'm not any wiser, not any less afraid, not any less retarded, not any different than the person I was when I woke up this morning.

And maybe that's the only denouement—or anti-denouement—of this recapitulation of my life: that I am just another retard among the millions of retards in the world, marching through life in my preprogrammed pointless way; and that the only thing that separates me from the masses—and from those gringos at the bar in Panama City—is not my secretive ways, but my efforts to be kind. Anyone can keep their sexuality private. But it takes conscious thought to stop the flow of "normal" thoughts and "normal" events and show some kindness, first to yourself and then to everyone else. Being kind is the only thing that keeps it all from being pointless.

I keep going back to the opening lines of the Dhammapada:

> *All experience is preceded by mind,*
> *Led by mind,*
> *Made by mind.*
> *Speak or act with a corrupt mind and suffering follows*
> *as the cart wheel follows the ox;*
> *Speak or act with a peaceful mind and happiness follows*
> *like a shadow that never departs.*

I don't think that means I have to be any less discerning. How those gringos denigrate those barroom hookers with their comments and their catcalls is still wrong and shameful. But if I cannot help my nature (and I can't), then it must be equally true that they cannot help their nature. And the suffering they will experience—the alienation, the lack of connection, the shallowness of their relationships—follows their actions just as much as those same consequences follow my own actions. We all suffer from disconnection from others because we all think of ourselves as disconnected from others. We are alone because we think we are alone.

That's the great paradox of change, you know: That we cannot change ourselves until we realize that we cannot change. Maybe that's why Freud said that the only goal of therapy was understanding and self-acceptance. Only when we realize that we are absolutely stuck in the same repetitive neurotic pattern, inherited from our DNA and our experiences and our parents and our parents' parents; only when we realize we are stuck on the Wheel of Life, on whatever bardo we were born into, only when we realize there is nothing we can do to change how our mind works, how we are programmed, how we automatically jump every time the bell rings... only when we finally accept that we are just fucking retarded can we stop and take a breath and maybe... maybe... do one kind thing for someone else. And maybe that one kind thing will make them pause for just a second, add one grain of sand to their kindness balance, and maybe they will act more kindly to someone else in turn... I don't know. That is simply the best I can figure. I do not have the power (nor the desire) to change myself. Already I've been googling different cities in Europe to see if there are any new sex clubs, any new bathhouses. I know that the blind pursuit of pleasure doesn't lead anywhere. But I'm not going to change—because my mind has told me all my life that this is the most I am entitled to. But it will be interesting to see, as a result of being kinder to myself and others, whether life will present me with other alternatives, will open up new relationships or a new community, or whether I will just end up feeling happier. Maybe kindness is the philosopher's stone that the Alchemists were searching for—the elixir of life that can transform my psychological lead into gold. Maybe the great karmic wheel has sent me back to learn a lesson. Or maybe I chose to be reborn as a human as part of a cosmic game.

Maybe I'm just a god who came back to earth to learn how to love.

—FIN—

ABOUT THE AUTHOR

Robert Rahula was born in Spain to an American father and Spanish mother, but grew up in Virginia on the farm of his paternal grandparents. He returned to Menorca, Spain, in the 1960s to pursue his writing career. These days he travels in Europe, Central and South America for several months a year, giving readings and lectures, and spends the rest of his time writing, dividing his time between Spain and the United States.

Over the past thirty years, Robert has published dozens books of prose and poetry in Spain and in the United States. While he remains relatively undiscovered in the United States, he is revered in Spain as the founder of the "portilla" style of popular Spanish poetry: non-metered fluid verse that deals with love, loss, bisexuality, separateness, and growing older.

www.ingramcontent.com/pod-product-compliance
Lightning Source LLC
Chambersburg PA
CBHW052051070526
44584CB00017B/2123